Orson Squire Fowler

Matrimony

Phrenology and Physiology Applied to the Selection of Congenial

Companions for Life

Orson Squire Fowler

Matrimony
Phrenology and Physiology Applied to the Selection of Congenial Companions for Life

ISBN/EAN: 9783337811716

Printed in Europe, USA, Canada, Australia, Japan

Cover: Foto ©Suzi / pixelio.de

More available books at **www.hansebooks.com**

MATRIMONY;

OR,

PHRENOLOGY AND PHYSIOLOGY.

MATRIMONY;

OR,

PHRENOLOGY AND PHYSIOLOGY

APPLIED TO THE SELECTION OF CONGENIAL
COMPANIONS FOR LIFE.

INCLUDING

DIRECTIONS TO THE MARRIED

FOR LIVING AFFECTIONATELY AND HAPPILY.

BY

O. S. FOWLER.

———

JOHN HEYWOOD,
DEANSGATE AND RIDGEFIELD, MANCHESTER;
AND 11, PATERNOSTER BUILDINGS,
LONDON.
1885.

MATRIMONY;

OR,

PHRENOLOGY AND PHYSIOLOGY

APPLIED TO THE SELECTION OF CONGENIAL PARTNERS FOR LIFE ; INCLUDING
DIRECTIONS TO THE MARRIED FOR LIVING TOGETHER
AFFECTIONATELY AND HAPPILY.

————•••◆•———

MAN is eminently a SOCIAL being. This is evinced by his phrenological
developments, and by his disposition to congregate and form friendships. His
social affections lie at the very *basis* of his virtue and happiness. Parental
and connubial love are among the highest species of enjoyment belonging to
his nature ; while blighted affections and family dissensions bear the most
bitter fruits he can taste—the former placing its happy possessor almost above
the reach of trouble ; and the latter, being the canker-worm of his every pleasure. The operation of no element of his character is more conducive to
virtue or happiness, and the destruction of none would leave him more utterly
desolate and wretched.

How beautiful, how perfect throughout, are the domestic relations ! How
comfortable, how happy the family group gathered around their own fireside !
Husbands and wives quaffing the unalloyed sweets of connubial love—parents
protecting their children, and children nestling under the kind wings of
parental fondness—the parents providing for the children, and the children
serving the parents, and waiting upon one another—the elder children serving
the younger, and the younger clinging affectionately around the elder—the
whole family commingling their joys and sorrows ; all bound together by the
strongest and most tender ties of nature ; bestowing and receiving the
caresses of affection, and reciprocating a continued succession of kind offices.
If there be a green spot on our barren earth—a pleasant picture upon which
the fatigued eye can rest with delight—it is the *happy family*—it is domestic
bliss.

No other class of faculties exert a greater influence upon man than the
domestic ones. From no other fountain of his nature gushes forth a deeper,
broader, or more perpetual stream of happiness or misery.

Since the obedience or violation of those laws which govern these social
relations *cause* all this enjoyment or suffering, a *knowledge* of them is
ALL-IMPORTANT, especially to *young people*. Phrenology beautifully and
clearly unfolds and expounds these laws.

But, in order fully to appreciate the vast power of the social faculties, or
understand those laws which govern their action, we must briefly *analyse*
them. They are—

AMATIVENESS:

Reciprocal attachment and LOVE *of the* SEXES *for each other.*

Its primary function is connubial love. From it mainly spring those feelings which exist between the sexes as such, and result in marriage and offspring. Combined with the higher sentiments, it gives rise to all those reciprocal kind feelings and nameless courtesies which each sex manifests towards the other; refining and elevating both, promoting gentility and politeness, and greatly increasing social and general happiness. So far from being gross and indelicate, its proper exercise is pure, chaste, virtuous, and even an ingredient in good manners. It is this which renders men always more polite towards women than to one another, and more refined in their society, and which makes woman more kind, grateful, genteel, and tender towards men than to women. It makes mothers love their sons more than their daughters, and causes fathers to be more attached to their daughters. Man's endearing recollections of his mother or wife form his most powerful incentives to virtue, study, and good deeds, as well as the most powerful restraints upon his vicious inclinations; and in proportion as a young man is dutiful and affectionate to his *mother* will he be fond of his *wife,* for this faculty is the parent of both.

Those in whom it is large and active are alive to the personal charms and mental accomplishments of the other sex; ardent admirers of their beautiful forms, graceful movements, elegant manners, soft and winning tones, looks, accents, &c., seek and enjoy their society; easily reciprocate fond looks and feelings with them; create favourable impressions, and kindle in them emotions of friendship, or the passion of love; and, with Adhesiveness (or Friendship*) large, are inclined to marry, and capable of the most devoted connubial love.

Those in whom it is deficient are proportionately cold-hearted, distant, and ill at ease in the society of the other sex; and less tender and affectionate, less soft and winning in their manners, less susceptible of connubial love, less inclined to marry, &c.

Its combinations, which so modify its action as actually to change its character from the best of feelings to the worst of passions, will be given after the other social faculties have been analysed.

Amativeness is supposed to be sub-divided; the lower and inner portions manifesting the mere animal passion, or physical love; the upper and outer portion, next to the ears, giving a disposition to caress, accompanied with pure platonic affection.

PHILOPROGENITIVENESS:

Parental love—Attachment to ONE'S *children—Love of children generally.*

Man enters the world in a condition truly helpless. Infants require a great amount of care and nursing. This infantile condition of man has its counterpart in this faculty. Without its stimulus to provide for and watch over infancy every infant must inevitably perish, and our race soon become extinct. No other faculty can fill its place, or accomplish its end. Infants cannot be

---

* Phrenology has suffered somewhat from the attempt of its founders to put it on a *scientific* footing, and especially in giving *learned* names to the organs, instead of plain English names, expressive of the *function* of the faculties. In order to make himself more fully understood by all, the author will use the term Friendship instead of Adhesiveness; Parental Love instead of Philoprogenitiveness; Resistance instead of Combativeness; Appetite instead of Alimentiveness; Belief instead of Marvellousness; Observation instead of Individuality; and so with others, the names of which do not already express the function performed by the organ.

regarded as friends, so that Adhesiveness cannot help them. Though Causality might devise ways and means for their relief and comfort, yet it would not execute them ; and though Benevolence might do something, yet it would be far too little for their physical salvation or for their moral and intellectual cultivation ; for how many are there who are kind to adults, but unwilling to be burdened with the care of children ?

These vexatious and expensive little creatures are far more likely to array Combativeness, Destructiveness, Acquisitiveness, &c., *against* them, than to enlist Benevolence or any other faculty in their behalf. If parents were not endowed with a faculty *expressly* adapted to the nursing and training of children, their burden would be intolerable. But this faculty not only casts into the shade all the toil, trouble, and expense they cause, but even lacerates the parental heart with the keenest pangs when death tears parents and children asunder. It renders children the richest treasure that parents possess ; an object for which they willingly labour, sacrifice, and suffer more than for all others. It sweetens their toils by day, and their watchfulness by night. Scarcely any loss equals that of children. But why? Let the amount of brain allotted to this faculty, especially in *mothers*, answer.

The primary distinctive function of this organ is PARENTAL LOVE—attachment to one's own children ; and the more helpless the child, the more vigorous its action. It also extends to grandchildren, and the children of others ; yet its power is far less towards them than towards one's own children. None but parents can ever know the genuine *feelings* of a parent's heart. Love of children is still further heightened by their being born of a wife, or begotten by a husband, whom we dearly love. Hence children are regarded as "the dear pledges of connubial love," because Parental Love is located by the side of Connubial Love ; so that the exercise of either naturally excites that of the other.*

The duties and relations of mothers to their children require a much stronger development of this faculty in woman than in man. Accordingly, it is much larger in females than in males. This increased size of the organ, and greater power of feeling in woman, and their adaptation to the far greater demand made upon her by her offspring, not only evince the truth of Phrenology, by showing it to harmonise with nature, but show that upon *her* devolve more of the nursing, training, and early education of children, than upon man. They peculiarly adapt women to develop the minds and train the feelings of children ; and hence teachers of little children should always be *females*. Woman's delicacy of feeling and quickness of perception ; her tenderness and willingness to do and to suffer ; her intuitive knowledge of the little wants of children ; her gentleness and playfulness peculiarly adapt her to expand the tender germ of their intellect ; to train their feelings, and to instill into their susceptible hearts the first principles of moral rectitude ; to cultivate benevolence and piety ; to develop their affections, and to start the youthful traveller in the paths of virtue and intelligence.

---

* This analysis renders the inference clear and forcible that parents should nurse and educate their own children. What end in life is more important? Is it not infinitely more so than making money, or acquiring fame or office? If parents cannot do all they desire, and yet find time to care for and educate their children, let them hire the other things done, while *they themselves*, not oversee, but actually train and educate their own children. If they do not know enough, or if they cannot afford the time, they are bound, by the most sacred obligations of our nature, not to *become* parents. Getting children nursed out ; sending them to school just to be rid of them : employing "wet nurses," and pretending to be too great a lady to nurse or tend one's own children, is a breach of nature's laws, and will inevitably incur the consequent penalties. Strange ! that mothers will ruin their children, and violate their natures, just to be fashionable. Let those who cannot get their children taken care of and educated count this their gain, and those who employ low, ignorant, or vicious nurses—a practice as common as it is reprehensible—bear in mind the principle brought to view in the text, and also remember that these grovelling and often immoral associations are sure to pollute their children. But more of this in my work on "Phrenology applied to Education and Self-Improvement," in which mothers are presented with a recipe for finding time to educate their own children.

The great development of this organ in woman, rendering her principal duty her greatest pleasure, is a beautiful instance of Divine wisdom and benevolence. But this delightful task conceded by all to woman during *infancy* is too soon wrested from her hands. Mothers should be their children's chief instructors. Happy would it be for families, happy for society, if woman were to devote herself more exclusively to these duties. To you, young ladies—ye future mothers of our race—do we look for the faithful performance of this momentous duty. You are to form the intellectual and moral character of our race, and should prepare yourselves accordingly. Is it right, then—does it comport with this great end of your being—that your time should be spent in following the fashions, in acquiring the "*graces*" (as this fashionable foolery is called), or in fashionable boarding schools, where not a thing is thought of appertaining to a preparation for becoming wives and mothers? Before you think of receiving a single attention from a gentleman, see to it, I beseech you, for *his* sake, for your *own* sake, for the sake of your *offspring*, that you fit yourselves to develop all the *physical*, the *moral*, and the *intellectual* capacities of children.

This powerful development in woman renders it evident that the primary object of female education should be to fit young ladies for the station of *wives* and *mothers*. But more will be seen in reference to female education in another portion of the work.

ADHESIVENESS.

Friendship—the SOCIAL *feeling—love of society—desire and ability to form attachments, congregate, associate, visit, and entertain friends, &c.*

If man had been created a lonely, unsocial, solitary being, nearly half his faculties, having nothing to excite them to action, would have lain dormant, and the remainder would have been but feebly exercised. The activity of a faculty in *one* naturally excites the same faculty in those around him. Hence, without the element of Friendship to bring mankind together into associations, neighbourhoods, families, &c., they could have had no opportunity for the exercise of Language, Ambition, Imitation, and many other faculties, and but little opportunity for that of Kindness, Justice, &c.; and all the remainder would have been far less efficient and pleasurable than now. Without this arrangement, co-partnerships, and those public and private works which require the combined labour and resources of more than one individual for their completion, would have remained unknown, and the selfish propensities have rendered all men Ishmaelites—turning every man's hand against his neighbour, rendering each most hateful to all; kindling rising jealousies, animosities, &c., into burning flames; and for ever blotting out the pleasant smile of glowing friendship, the cordial greeting of old associates, and that silent flow of perpetual happiness which springs from being in the company of those we like.

The *young* form attachments much more readily than those who are older, partly because the latter become hardened by frequent disappointments in finding supposed friends unfaithful, and partly because they have been longer separated from the friends of their youth. This blunting of the fine glowing feelings of friendship is certainly most unfortunate. Friendship should be regarded as *most sacred*, and never to be trifled with. We should do almost anything sooner than violate this feeling. Friends should bear and forbear much, at least, until they are *certain* that a supposed injury or unjust remark was *premeditated*. *Then*, when friendship is thus violated, we should think no more of our former friend, not even enough to hate him. Dwell not upon the injuries done to you; banish both them and the traitor from your mind, and let him be to you as though you had never known him. Dwelling upon broken faith only still farther wounds and blunts the feeling of genuine friendship. Never *form* friendships where there is much danger of their being broken, and never break them unless the occasion is most aggravating and intentionally given. Let friends try to make up *little* differences as soon as possible.*

These remarks apply with redoubled power to members of the same family. Let parents cultivate affection for one another in their children, and let brothers and sisters separate as little as possible, corresponding much, and, if possible, never allow a breach to be made in their attachments. Add continually new fuel to the old fire of family friendship. Let the right of *hospitality* be extended more often than it now is, and let friends entertain friends around the family board as often as possible, instead of allowing them to eat their unsocial fare at the public hotel. We have too little of the good old Yankee custom of *"Cousining,"* and of English hospitality, and spend far too little time in making and receiving *social visits.* These *formal, polite* calls are perfect nuisances. They are to friendship what the smut is to the grain—poisonous. True friendship knows no *formality.*

UNION FOR LIFE.

There is little doubt of the existence of another faculty, located between Adhesiveness and Amativeness, which disposes husbands and wives in whom it is *large* and *active* to be *always together.* The absence of their companion, even for an hour, is quite painful. They feel as though the time spent away from them was so much of their existence lost. It is developed before Amativeness appears, and hence this Union is often formed in childhood. It purifies and refines the sentiment of love; desires to caress and be caressed; and is the soul and centre of connubial love; creating that *union,* that *oneness* of feeling, that harmony of spirit, and that *flowing together* of soul, which constitute true conjugal affection. It is very reluctant to fasten upon more than one, and that one the first love.

I have seen several striking proofs and illustrations of the existence of this faculty, and the location of its organ. I know a lady in whom both are marked, who, whenever her husband is about to leave her for a few days, feels an acute pain in that organ. When she pointed out the location of this pain, and stated that it always accompanied the absence of her husband, I saw that it belonged to neither Adhesiveness nor Amativeness, but was located *between* the two. As the intensity of the pain rendered this matter certain, I surmised the existence of another organ, and, two years afterwards, found it confirmed by observations made in France.

It is much larger and more active in woman than in man, which causes and accounts for the far greater power and intensity of woman's love than that of man's.

INHABITIVENESS:

Or, love of HOME, *and the* DOMICILE *of both childhood and after-life; attachment to the* PLACE *where one lives or has lived; unwillingness to change it; desire to locate and remain permanently, in one habitation, and to* OWN *and* IMPROVE *a homestead—Patriotism.*

Home, home! sweet, sweet home!
There's no place like home.

The advantages of having a permanent HOME, and the evils and losses consequent upon *changing* it,† are both very great: "Three moves," it is said,

---

* I have seen a young man rendered crazy, and thrown into a perfect frenzy of excitement by being imposed upon by a supposed friend—one, too, of his own sex. He appeared very much like those who have been recently disappointed in love.

† It is estimated that the expense of moving on the 1st of May, in the city of New York alone, exceeds twenty-five thousand dollars

" are as bad as a fire." Those who have homes of their *own*, be they ever so homely, are comparatively rich. They feel that no crusty landlord can turn them homeless into the streets, or sell their furniture at an auction for rent. Rent-days come and go unheeded, and the domestic affections have full scope for delightful exercise. Every married man is bound by this *inhabitive* law of his nature, as well as in duty to his family, to *own* a house and garden plot ; and every wife is bound by the same law and duty to render that home as agreeable as possible.

The prevalent practice of *renting* houses violates this law and arrangement of man's domestic nature, and must necessarily produce evil to both owner and tenant. This is established by facts as well as theory ; for what observer is not at once struck with the general fact that landlords improve their houses only to raise their rents, and charge enormously for every additional convenience ; and that tenants will not make improvements because they intend soon to "move." All permanent improvements, such as fertilising or beautifying a garden, rearing fruit trees of various kinds, setting out a shrubbery, &c., raising stock, and getting conveniences and comforts for a family around you, require a succession of years ; tenants, therefore, are compelled to do without them. If they wish fruit or vegetables, instead of plucking the fully ripe cherry, the delicious peach or pear, and the ever-varying fruits of the seasons, and sitting down quietly to enjoy them "under their own vine and fig-tree," by which their relish would be doubled, they are obliged to take their up hard-earned money, pay a four-fold price in the market, and, after all, take with articles that are green, withered, or stale ; it being the universal custom to pluck fruit for the market before it is ripe, so that it may keep the longer, and not spoil by being transported. Who has not tasted the difference in eatables fresh from the garden, compared with those purchased in the market ? Again : market men, being generally too poor to own land, are obliged to demand high prices in order to cover exorbitant rents, which furnishes an excuse for those who raise things for market on their own land to do the same. This, together with the market being forestalled by hucksters and speculators, increases the price of provisions so enormously that one dollar earned by those who *own* a house and a bit of land brings more than five dollars earned by city tenants. What consummate folly, then, to emigrate from the country to cities because a dollar a week more wages may be given, when the increased expenses of rent, fuel, food, &c., are perhaps five times more than the additional earnings. This reveals one cause of the greater degree of poverty, privation, and suffering in the city than in the country.

Again : city tenants usually buy a small quantity at a time, such as a pound of meat, half a pound of sugar, a pint of milk, a halfpenny bunch of onions and radishes, an ounce of tea, a pound of flour, &c., and hence are obliged to pay double price, or at least all the difference between the wholesale and the retail prices, besides the increased price of articles in the city above that of the country ; while those who *own* land usually raise, or else lay in, their year's supply of provisions at the time of their production, and at a comparatively trifling cost. To this renting system mainly do we owe the exorbitant, but merely nominal price of "city property," the rents and the rise of the property combining to increase them; whereas were there but few tenants, the city prices would sink far below those demanded for country property, from which a living could be obtained. This *renting* system is one of the most efficient causes of "hard times" and distressing poverty. For a small room, too contracted to yield scarcely a comfort, and often in the basement or attic, many tenants are compelled to pay their hard-earned dollar every Saturday night, or be turned into the streets. This system has infused its baneful influences into nearly all the arrangements and relations of life. Indeed, so great and multifarious have its evils become, that they will compel men ere long to abandon it, and *buy* a poorer house in preference to *renting* a better one. Rents will then fall, and landlords be losers. To own the house you *live* in is enough ; owning more will injure all concerned.

This faculty and its combinations plainly indicate that the prevalent practice of " boarding" is not the most profitable or agreeable. The *social* feelings cannot find gratification or reciprocation. Besides, boarders frequently waste more than is necessary, so that boarding creates a selfish feeling where all should be harmony and friendship. And then to be sick in a boarding-house or tavern ! Let those who know its horrors bear witness. To be sick *at home*, with all the attentions that affection can bestow, is bad enough ; but to be sick among *strangers*, and have only such attention as *money* can procure, is the climax of wretchedness. Let young men whose circumstances compel them to board, choose some *good* family, and *identify* themselves with it, and cultivate the *social affections*, and then change the boarding-house for a home as soon as possible. Nor should young men leave their father's house as soon as they generally do : they should, in most cases, stay at home till they get homes of their own.

I have always observed that children who have lived in one dwelling, and especially on a farm, till they were fifteen, have this organ large, whereas it is small in those who have lived in *different* places during childhood. This says to parents, in the language of nature, " Make as few moves as possible, and generally keep your children at *home*."

It is also large in most farmers, and, with Approbativeness large, gives a kind of pride in having a *nice* farm, house, furniture, garden, &c., together with a disposition to *improve* one's residence. The lower portion of Parental love is supposed to create a fondness for pets, stock, and the young and tender of animals, with a disposition to improve their breed ; and the union of the two increases the charms of husbandry and farming. No life is so independent, so free from care, so healthy, or so favourable either to virtue or intellectual pursuits. If our farmers, instead of labouring with all their might to become *rich*, would labour just enough to earn a livelihood, and devote the remainder of their time to reading and study, no class of people on earth would be so happy, or moral, or talented. To leave the farm for the city or counting-room, evinces a species of folly bordering on derangement, or else sheer ignorance of the road to happiness. The best heads I have examined have been those of farmers ; and a majority of our great and good men will be found to have once followed the plough and reaped the harvest.

This organ also is supposed to be double : the inner portion creating attachment to the home of childhood, to the *family* domicile, to the stones, trees, and place of youth, and delighting to revisit them ; the outer creating patriotism and love of the more recent homestead, with unwillingness to "*move*."

THE COMBINATIONS OF THE SOCIAL FACULTIES.

Though the *individual* action of these social faculties is powerful, and productive of intense enjoyment or suffering, their *combinations* are much *more* so. Their *combinations* also account for the infinite diversity of tastes in the selection of friends and companions, and in the management of children.

Thus, those who have large Amativeness, combined with large Adhesiveness, not only love the other sex as such, but contract a strong *friendship* for them, and make them their warmest and most confidential *friends ;* and, with the addition of large " Union for Life," experience that *love* for some congenial spirit, some kindred soul, which makes " of twain one flesh," and perfectly unites "two willing hearts." Persons thus constituted are tender and affectionate as companions ; will mingle pure friendship with devoted love ; " cannot flourish alone," but will be inclined to love and marry young ; will invest the beloved one with almost angelic purity and perfection ; magnify their mental and moral charms, and overlook their defects ; feel happy in their company, but miserable without it ; freely unbosom every feeling ; communicate and

share every pain and pleasure ; and have the whole current of the other faculties enlisted in their behalf. With large Ideality and the mental temperament
added, they will experience a purity, a devotion, a fervour, an elevation, and
intensity, and even *ecstasy* of love well nigh romantic, especially the *first* love.
They fasten upon *mental* and *moral*, instead of *personal* charms, or rather
blend the two.   They can fall in love only with one who combines good looks
with refinement, good manners, and much delicacy of feeling ; will be soon
disgusted with what is improper, not in good taste, coarse, or vulgar in the
person, dress, manners, conversation, &c., of the sex, but exceedingly pleased
with the opposite qualities ; will express love in a refined, delicate, and accept-
able manner ; be fond of poetry, tales, romances, and the sentimental.   With
Parental Love also large, they will be eminently qualified to enjoy the domestic
relations of companions and parents ; be as happy in the family relations as
they can be in any other, and stay from home only when compelled.   When
Inhabitiveness is large, they will travel half the night to be at home the other
half ; sleep poorly from home ; and remove only when they cannot well avoid
it.   With large Firmness and Conscientiousness added to this combination,
they will be constant, and keep the marriage relations inviolate, regarding
them as the most sacred feelings of our nature.   With large Combativeness
added, they will defend the object loved with much spirit, and indignantly
resent scandals or indignities offered them.   With large Approbativeness
added, they will hear them praised with delight, and greatly enjoy their
approval, but be cut to the heart by their reproaches.   If moderate or small
Self-esteem, and large Ideality, and only average or full Conscientiousness and
Causality be added, they will be too ready to follow the fashions demanded by
the other sex, and too sensitive to their censure—a combination too common
in women.   With large Secretiveness and Cautiousness, they will *feel* much
more affection than is expressed, appearing indifferent, especially at first, or
till the other party is committed ; and perhaps not bring matters to a direct
issue till too late ; but with Secretiveness only moderate or small, they will
throw wide open the portal of the heart ; freely showing in every look, word
and action all the love they feel.   With Firmness, Self-esteem, and Friendship
all large, they will not be subdued by love, however powerful, nor be humble
or servile in this matter ; but bear its interruption with fortitude ; and will be
the reverse when Self-esteem, Firmness, and Combativeness are only moderate
or average.   With Causality and the head only moderate or average in size, the
vital or mental temperament predominant, and Adhesiveness, Approbativeness
and Ideality large or very large, they will prefer the company of the fashionable, dressy, gay, superficial, witty, showy, &c., of the other sex, and love to
indulge in small talk with them, and love and marry those of this class.   With
the moral faculties predominant, they will choose the virtuous, moral, devout,
and religious for friends and companions.   With the intellectual organs large
or very large, they can admire and love only those who are intellectual,
sensible, and literary.   They will almost adore such, but be disgusted with the
opposite class.   With the vital or vital motive temperament predominant,
Ideality large or very large, and Causality and Conscientiousness only average
or moderate, they will be less particular as to their moral than their personal
charms ; will love the pretty face and figure last seen ; and have an attachment by no means exclusive ; courting many, rather than being satisfied with
individual attachment, and inclined to the merely animal gratification of
Amativeness ; and with large Language and Mirthfulness added, will delight
to joke with and about the other sex ; often be indelicate, fond of hearing if
not relating improper anecdotes about them, and of seeing vulgar prints, &c. ;
and with large Tune also added, be prone to sing objectionable songs, if not
inclined to revelry and profligacy ; and extremely liable to pervert Amativeness.   With large Acquisitiveness added, they will quite as soon marry
for money as for true love, especially after the first attachment has been
interrupted, &c.

But those in whom Amativeness is only moderate or small, the mental temperament predominant, and the moral faculties more active than the propensities, will not love or marry young, but will have more friendship and pure platonic affection than animal feeling, &c.

These combinations are given mainly as a sample of the others, and also to illustrate the law of love, and account for different matrimonial tastes. Additional ones will be found in the author's work on Phrenology.

LOCATION OF THE SOCIAL ORGANS.

The social organs are located together, in a kind of *family group*, in the back and lower portions of the head, behind the ears. They predominate in the head of an affectionate female. This is the usual form of the female head, and the social faculties constitute the predominant quality of the female character; though Amativeness is usually smaller in women than in men. These organs, when very large and active, elongate the head backwards, behind the ears, and their activity causes the head to recline directly back towards the spine. Those who have a slim neck, and a head projecting behind the ears, but narrrow at its junction at the back of the neck, are susceptible of much purity and tenderness of love, which will be founded in friendship and union of soul more than in animal passion; but those whose heads are broad between the ears at their union with the back of the neck, and the back parts of whose heads do not project much behind the neck, or are nearly on a line with it, will have more animal passion than pure affection. Though a full development of Amativeness is important in a companion, yet large Friendship and high moral faculties are quite as much so.

In this family group there may be two or more additional organs, one of which is doubtless located between Friendship and the upper part of Parental Love, and creates attachment to *keepsakes*, or gifts presented by friends; to old household furniture which has descended from parents to children; also to things long used. Another is probably located at the sides of Parental Love, which experiences the emotion of FILIAL LOVE, causing children to love, obey, and wait upon their parents; to sit at the feet of age and experience, and learn lessons of wisdom, or listen to their stories, follow their counsels, especially those of parents; and to cherish for parents that filial affection which delights to serve, nurse, love, and support them, and weeps over their departed spirits.

Let parents assiduously endeavour to cultivate filial affection in their children, and avoid everything calculated to wound or weaken it; and let children love their parents and cherish a disposition to serve them, so that when they become feeble or helpless, *Filial* Love may delight to *return* those unnumbered attentions received in childhood at the hands of *Parental Love!* How wise, how admirable this Parental Love! How beautiful, how perfect this Filial Attachment! The former giving parents the highest pleasure in nursing and providing for their children; and the latter, giving children equal pleasure in bestowing the same kind of attentions upon their parents; the former, softening the pillow of infancy, and supplying its wants; the latter, softening the pillow of age, and alleviating the infirmities of dotage, kindly proffering those attentions which Filial Love alone can bestow. What quality in youth is more praiseworthy, what recommendation for virtue or goodness more unequivocal, than devoted attachment to parents? How can vice or immorality dwell in a bosom filled with love and devotedness to an aged needy parent? What is more meritorious, or what yields a richer harvest of happiness than toiling to support an infirm parent?

But, on the other hand, how ungrateful, how utterly depraved, how superlatively wicked, must be those who neglect this pleasing duty of taking care of their parents, or who let them want; or, above all, who desire their death, or

hasten it by neglect or abuse, in order the sooner to inherit their patrimony !
Give me the glorious privilege of cherishing my dearly beloved parents ; and,
at last, when their days are all numbered, let them breathe their last in my
arms, as I myself desire to do in those of my children ; and let this family
feeling be cherished from generation to generation.

AMOUNT OF BRAIN ALLOTTED TO THE SOCIAL ORGANS.

Nothing exhibits the power and energy of these social faculties, or the
importance of their proper exercise in a more striking light than the *great
amount of brain allotted to their organs*, which averages from one-twelfth to
one-sixth of the whole.   Do not, on any account, marry one, the back of whose
head indicates predominant Amativeness.   Still, an *ample* development
behind the ears is a primary and most important requisite in a companion
and parent.   Those in whom it is deficient will never enjoy a family, nor
render it happy.

It is a well established principle of phrenology that, activity and other
things being equal, the larger the amount of brain called into action, the greater
will be the enjoyment or suffering experienced.   This, in part, explains the
immense power of the social feelings over the happiness and misery of mankind.   And this power is greatly augmented by their *location*, or physiological
relation to the other portions of the brain—it being directly calculated to
throw much of the latter into a state analogous to their own.   Hence the
neutral action of the social feelings tends to quiet all the others, which is
highly promotive of virtue and enjoyment ; but their *fevered* or *inflamed*
condition tends to inflame the whole brain, especially the *animal propensities*,
among which they are located, which causes vice and misery.   This inflamma-
tion renders those recently disappointed in love irritable, fault-finding, and
displeased with everything and everybody, and unfit for study or the
advantageous exercise of intellect ; because their whole brain and mind are
thrown into violent commotion, and all their animal propensities are highly
excited.   Nothing excites Combativeness and Destructiveness to so high a
pitch of indignation, if not revenge, as to be cut out or "crossed in love;" or
to have a supposed friend prove untrue ; or to lose a child, companion, or
friend ; or any other interruption of the social feelings.

Why are duels fought, and more animosities engendered, by interruptions
in love, and consequent jealousy, than by any other cause ? Let the juxta-
position of the organs of Love and Resistance answer. Even the moral and
religious organs are greatly disturbed thereby. On the other hand, many
readers can bear experimental witness to that peace of mind, that delightful
composure, that happy state of feeling which follows marriage, or the final and
favourable adjustment of reciprocated love.   These, and kindred states of
mind, are caused, and beautifully accounted for, by this principle.

And what is more, the facility and power with which these faculties *combine*,
individually and collectively, with each and all the other faculties, is greater
than that with which any other classes combine. This greatly augments their
power of exciting all the other faculties to the highest pitch of pleasurable or
painful action, accordingly as they are properly or improperly placed ; so that
their condition reciprocally affects, if it does not go far actually to control, that
of the balance of the brain, and with it, the state of the mind ; and they
proportionally hold the keys of our happiness or misery.

To illustrate : Though the meal eaten alone may gratify appetite, yet, even
the pleasures of the palate are greatly augmented by the exquisite satisfaction
derived from our own table surrounded by our family and friends. This

increased enjoyment promotes digestion and health, which redoubles all our enjoyments, besides prolonging life.*

Combativeness, or the element of resistance, is called into more powerful action by indignities offered to one's family, than by being cheated, or repro. ched, or by any other imposition that can be practised upon one's self. What husband or wife will not resent an indignity offered to a wife or daughter sooner than one offered to himself? Our heroic fathers, actuated mainly by love of their families, and to protect their firesides, braved every danger, endured every privation, and conquered the conquerors of the world. To this combination mainly do we owe our ever glorious independence. This principle holds equally true of Destructiveness and Secretiveness.

Marriage doubles and quadruples the energy of Acquisitiveness. Many young men, who, before becoming husbands and fathers, are prodigal of their time and lavish of their money, spending much of both in what injures instead of benefits them, after marriage save everything, and practice rigid economy, besides converting every hour to some useful purpose. The best recipe for becoming wealthy is to marry, not a rich, but a *frugal* companion. Marriage renders a home necessary, and greatly increases efforts to provide one.

Cautiousness is agreeably and continually excited by the cares of a family— by watching over children, and providing for their present and prospective wants; whilst Self-esteem affords parents as much patriarchal pleasure in governing their household as it does a king in ruling his kingdom. The agreeable exercise of Acquisitiveness greatly increases this delight in those who have to say that they *own* a house, and land enough to live upon; so that they are independent, can defy the banks and hard times, and owe no man anything.

Approbativeness, or love of the good opinion of others, in the unmarried is confined mainly to *themselves;* that of parents reverts to their children. The single lady is pleased with marks of commendation bestowed upon her dress, appearance, attainments, and things appertaining to *herself;* while the mother is doubly delighted with praises bestowed upon her darling *child*, taking more pride in adorning its person and improving its mind, than she ever took in regard to herself. Praises bestowed upon *it* sound more sweetly in her ear, and awaken more thrilling emotion in her bosom, than those bestowed upon herself ever had the power of doing; because the latter strike but the single chord of Approbativeness, while praises bestowed upon the *child* sweep harmoniously the *two* chords of Approbativeness and Parental Love combined, thereby more than doubling her pleasure, and opening the shortest and surest way of access to the goodwill of parents. What but this powerful combination, uncontrolled, could produce that excessive and almost sickening parental vanity which many parents lavish upon their children, or account for their conceit that *their* children excel those of most others, of which the majority of parents are guilty?

The family affords Conscientiousness ample scope for delightful exercise in dealing out even-handed *justice* to all, and in implanting in the tender minds of their children lessons of *duty* and the principles of *right;* while Hope feasts itself upon the promises their expanding intellects afford of dawning talents,

---

* An extensive census taken in England, for the purpose of comparing the ages of a specified number of married persons of both sexes with the same number of those who were single, shows that 78 married men attain the age of forty, while 41 bachelors attain the same age. As age advances, the difference is still more striking. At sixty, there are 98 married men alive to only 22 unmarried, or four-and-a-half to one. At seventy, there are only 11 bachelors alive, to 27 married men, or nearly three to one; and at ninety, there are 9 married men to three bachelors. Nearly the same rule holds good with regard to the female sex. Married women, at the age of thirty, on an average, may expect to live thirty-six years longer, but the unmarried only thirty (that is, one-fifth less). Of those who attain the age of forty-five, there are 72 married women alive for 52 single ladies, the difference being nearly one-third. Beyond all doubt there is something in marriage highly calculated, in itself, both to prolong life, and to render that life more peaceful and happy.

virtue, and honour—transporting parental love in view of the brightening prospects of their coming prosperity, as well as of the enjoyments yet to be realised in the family circle.

To him who delights in prayer and praise to God, the exercise of Veneration may yield a rich harvest of pure and exalted pleasure ; but it is when offering the morning and evening sacrifice of prayer and thanksgiving around the FAMILY altar—when praying with the family for blessings *upon* the family — that this faculty is kindled up to its most devout and fervent action ; melting the heart, purifying the soul, and reforming the conduct. How much more gratifying to go to church or chapel in *company* than alone ! This increase of pleasure has its origin in the *combination* of Veneration and these Social Faculties. Marvellousness, also, delights to commit and commend those objects of affection to the merciful protection and gracious guidance of an all-wise and over-ruling Providence.

Though the exercise of Benevolence towards strangers, or even brutes, gives a great amount of real pleasure, yet we feel double gratification in conferring favours upon those we love. The family presents *many* an opportunity for doing little acts of kindness, where the world at large affords *one*.   Indeed, it enables us to be doing and receiving an almost *continued succession* of kind offices, perhaps trifling in themselves, but great in their aggregate, and highly promotive of reciprocal good feeling. Children can gratify Imitation by taking pattern from their beloved and venerated parents ; while the wife can indulge her Ideality and Order in keeping the house and children neat, tidy, and clean, and in cultivating vines, flowers, &c.* The family also affords the wife an admirable opportunity to exercise her Constructiveness—which is called into action in nearly everything done with the hands—in making and repairing garments and conveniences for those she loves, and at the same time endearing herself to her husband by gratifying his Acquisitiveness, in saving many a tailor's bill, &c. ; while *he* will find *his* Constructiveness agreeably exercised in fixing up things, and making conveniences about the house, repairing a door, inserting a broken glass, &c, as well as in the daily labour of his hands in their support.

With all the freedom allowed in the family circle, Mirthfulness can let fly its sprightly jokes, its agreeable sallies of wit, and its tart repartees, without the least fear of giving offence, or any of that studied guardedness or artificial precision required among others. The Language and Eventuality of parents and grandparents find frequent and delightful exercise in recounting to their young and eager listeners the incidents of bygone days, and the history and genealogy of their ancestors, and in telling or reading to them stories calcula-ted to strengthen their memories and improve their morals ; while the children, in return, also indulge *their* Language in their incessant prattle.

It is in the family circle, also, that Tune can exert its powerful charms by striking up a cheerful lay, and giving expression to buoyant, elastic feeling in unreserved strains of thrilling melody and pathos. How exalted a source of pleasure is music ! How powerful an instrument of good or evil—of moral purity or debasement—of subduing unruly passions and harmonising all the discordant faculties ! To enliven and make cheerful the *home;* to throw a charm around the *fireside;* to dispel the vexations and disappointments of unpropitious business, and make a family happy, is its peculiar prerogative. What will quell the turbulent temper of a child, or assuage the irritability of a husband, or soothe his depressed spirits as he returns home disappointed, or

---

* Every good wife will gladly improve every opportunity to adorn her house, especially with *natural* charms, and render it as pleasant and agreeable as possible. This seems to be one im-portant and leading duty, or rather pleasure, of a wife and mother ; and yet that one is too much neglected.   Let every wife have her flower garden, her arbour, her plants, and shrubbery, and by throwing those little charms and niceties around "home" which the hand and the taste of woman alone can impart, give to it a peculiar and pleasant attraction. But more on this point elsewhere.

weary, or angry, from the business of the day, so soon as to hear his wife or daughter strike up a cheerful lay, or play a favourite tune? Its power in this respect is underrated, and too seldom applied, and *modern* music is often too artificial to awaken or divert the feelings.*

How vast the sum total of that quiet stream of the purest, sweetest enjoyments flowing almost continually from the affectionate and happy family circle, with their comfortable fire blazing before them, and the means at hand of gratifying every returning want; including their agreeable conversation, pouring incessantly from every mouth; the pleasant chit-chat of the table and parlour, and that ceaseless prattle provoked by the domestic feelings and family arrangements!

Here, also, Order has a wide field for delightful exercise, by having a place for everything, and everything in its place, so as to have things forthcoming at a moment's call; and Time, by having a time for everything, and everything in its season; meals punctual, and all at their meals at the same time, &c. Here, too, Causality and the Social Faculties combine with Benevolence in giving advice, and contriving and arranging matters for their comfort; with Language or Comparison, in explaining their conclusions, and in asking and answering questions; with Acquisitiveness, in devising and executing ways and means of augmenting their estate; with Cautiousness, in foreseeing danger and providing against it, and securing their good; and so of other combinations. In short, what motive equals that of a needy or dependent family for putting the Causality of parents upon the rack to invent a constant succession of devices for their relief—to sharpen up and call forth every power of the intellect, every energy of the body, every capacity of man, as well as to stir up every fountain of feeling in his soul?

But this delightful picture is often reversed; and then how changed the scene! How terrible when Combativeness, instead of *defending* the family group, is arrayed *against* it, and, calling Self-Esteem to its assistance, tyrannises over it, and rules with a rod of iron—when contention supplants protection, and angry looks dispel the smiles of affection—when their Approbativeness, instead of being gratified by commendation, is mortified by having their faults or follies exposed, or wounded by reproach—when Conscientiousness is offended by their unprincipled immoralities—when a want of Order or Punctuality in either incenses the Combativeness of the others—when Language, instead of engaging in agreeable conversation, is employed to mortify Approbativeness by administering reproaches or hurling reproof—when miserly Acquisitiveness, instead of making money to procure comforts for the family, arrays Combativeness against the family because they are expensive—in short, when the other faculties, instead of uniting with the Social Affections to make home a paradise and the family happy, are brought into collision with them, and make home a pandemonium—a real family hell—their sufferings are intolerable, and their warfare is perpetual, because the family relations bring them and keep them in constant contest, the most direct and powerful. Then it is that the stream of life is poisoned at its *fountain-head*, and made to send forth bitter waters continually. The very quintessence of misery consists in this collision, this warring of the faculties. As in the case of magnetic bodies, the *nearer* their contact the more powerful their attraction or *repulsion*, so the family relations bring every point in the character of each into direct unison with those of the others, or in flat opposition to them.

With great *emphasis*, therefore, I repeat this main proposition, that the influences of the domestic *organs* on the rest of the brain, and of the social *faculties* on the other mental powers, are so direct and reciprocal, that their proper or improper exercise—their peaceful or disturbed action—throws the

---

* See the author's analysis of Tune, and criticisms on modern fashionable music, in his work on "Phrenology applied to Education and Self-Improvement."

whole brain and mind into a similar condition, forming a kind of *centre* of virtue and happiness, or of vice and misery. Is a man but happy in the *domestic* relations, he is happy everywhere, in spite of all the evils that can assail him. What though the storms of adversity beat violently upon his head, and misfortunes thicken upon him ; though the winds waft tidings of evil ; though scandal and reproach assail him from without, and sickness appears within ; though riches take to themselves wings and fly away, and his plans and prospects prove abortive ; if he but live affectionately with his wife, and see his children growing up to love and bless him, he is still happy. His joys are beyond the reach of misfortune.

But let a man be *miserable* at home ; let his wife prove unfaithful or unsocial, and his children become a disgrace to him ; and, though the breezes are wafting to him the wealth of the Indies—though the trumpet of fame is sounding his name throughout Christendom—though the sunshine of prosperity beams on his pathway with full effulgence, and success everywhere attends him—still a canker-worm is preying on his vitals—he is *most wretched*. His joys are rotten at the core ; his life is the dregs of bitterness. It is not in the power of either poverty, reproach, or misfortune to blast, or even embitter the fruits of domestic felicity ; while it *is* in the power of domestic discord or unhappiness to poison every sweet that either riches, or fame, or learning can bestow, and to mar even the consolations of religion. Let the blasting winds of adversity blow upon me a perfect hurricane of trouble ; let the afflictions of even Job be repeated upon me—only let me live in the bosom of my family, and let my wife and children be spared to greet me with the smiles and the kisses of affection, and my cup of pleasure is well nigh full.

And if these things be true of *man*, how much more so of WOMAN, whose *home* is the family, whose heart is tenderness, and whose very *being* is connubial and maternal love ! In her the blighted affections occasion the most bitter agony beneath the sun ! Indeed, words cannot express the amount either of the happiness which the social affections are capable of pouring into the human bosom, or the amount of sighs, and woes, and bitter sorrow with which they have the power to curse man. None but those who have tasted these things can know the full force of these remarks.

In proportion, therefore, to the power of these social faculties over the weal or woe of man is the importance of understanding and obeying the laws of their action ; that is, of properly placing and regulating our social affections If their exercise were productive of *good only*, it would be entirely proper for young people to fall in love and marry as they often now do—anyhow, just as it happens. It would also be proper for parents to make *pecuniary* matches. But as this is *not* the case, it becomes all candidates for marriage—nay, it is their *duty*, to place and exercise their social feelings with care. But many experience all the curses they are capable of inflicting—curses proportionate to the blessings they are capable of conferring. *Why* is this ? Is it *unavoidable?* This would be charging *God* foolishly, and blaming him for our own folly and stupidness. Cannot all be happy in the domestic relations? Is not happiness here, like happiness everywhere else, the result of the action of certain fixed and invariable laws? And is not this equally the case in regard to domestic *misery?* By applying to yourself causes productive of happiness, you will be happy ; but by applying opposite causes, you have opposite results. And these causes are mostly in your own hands, so that all have it in their power to say whether they will enjoy domestic life, or endure it, or have a bitter-sweet.

The question then returns with redoubled force—HOW can we so place and regulate our social affections as to secure all the blessings they are designed and adapted to yield ? and HOW avoid all the evils they are capable of inflicting ? Phrenology kindly replies. It unfolds the laws of man's social nature, on the observance or violation of which these momentous results depend. It even goes farther—it shows us how to obey them. Mark well its teachings, observe and follow its directions, and you will drink in the joys designed by nature to flow from married life.

In order to marry so as to be happy in the domestic relations, we must first understand the precise thing to be done, and then the *means* of doing it. That thing is, to secure *Connubial* Love, which consists in the reciprocal exercise of the social faculties of two persons of opposite sexes, in harmony with all their other faculties. Union of soul, harmony of views and sentiments, congeniality of tastes and feelings, and a blending of the natures of both, so as to make 'twain one flesh,' is the *end* to be obtained. This is Love—that wonderful element of our nature which made Eleanor of Castile jeopardise her own life to save that of her beloved husband, Edward I., and suck the poison from his otherwise fatal wound ; which induced Gertrude Van der Wart to bid defiance to the ribaldry of the soldiers, and stand resolutely by the side of her racked and mangled husband during the whole of an awfully tempestuous night, soothing him by her sympathies, and sustaining him by her fortitude, till the cruel rack ended his life and sufferings together ; and which makes every fond wife and devoted husband willing, and even glad, to sacrifice their own ease and happiness, and rejoice in enduring toil, suffering, and self-denial, to relieve the sufferings and promote the happiness of their dearly-beloved companion.*

Having seen precisely *what requires to be done* in order to enjoy married life, the question returns as to the *means* of doing it. They are brief and simple, but plain.

SELECT A COMPANION WHOSE PHRENOLOGICAL DEVELOPMENTS AND TEMPERAMENT RESEMBLE YOUR OWN.

That is, select some one whose feelings, desires, sentiments, object, tastes, intellectual and moral qualities, in all their *leading* elements, &c., *harmonise* with your own.† The fundamental law of both love and friendship is this : *We become attached to those whose qualities of intellect and feeling resemble our own.* The reason is, that as the proper exercise of every faculty gives pleasure, and as the active faculties of each excite the same faculties of the other, those whose objects, sentiments, and other qualities resemble our own, most powerfully excite, and thereby gratify our *own* organs, while ours at the same time *harmonise* with theirs, and thus give them the greatest amount of pleasure. Thus, if your Conscientiousness, or sense of *justice* be strong, the same faculty

---

* There are two kinds of love—the one healthy, the other sickly ; the one virtuous and elevating, the other questionable ; the one strong and natural, and governed by judgment ; the other, a greenhouse exotic, governing the intellect, springing up before its time, and bearing unripe, unhealthy fruit. Persons afflicted with this unnatural parasite are said to be "love-sick," and sick enough it sometimes makes its youthful victims. This kind of love will frequently be found described in novels, and its workings seen in young people in high life, improperly so called, for it afflicts those of a nervous temperament and sentimental cast of mind most grievously. Those who are above labour, who are too good to mingle with the middle classes, or engage in any useful occupation ; who have little to do except attend balls and parties, to dress in the height of the fashion, thumb the piano, and such high-life occupations ; those whose parents roll in luxury, or live in affluence ; those boys and girls whose worth is neither in their heads nor hearts, but in their fathers' name and pockets, are most apt to be attacked by this "love-sickness." They are usually "smitten" with it at a party, or dance, or sail ; they exchange kisses, &c., and conclude by proposing and accepting, and sending for the parson. This love-sick kind of feeling is much more prevalent in the city than in the country, and attacks its victims there much earlier, besides rendering them, if possible, still more soft and sickish there than elsewhere ; and it is one of the principal causes of so many unhappy marriages.

The other kind of love appears in our working, substantial swains and dames, who think little and care less about love and matrimony till their physical powers are developed, their characters and judgments matured, and their intellects sufficiently unfolded to guide their love understandingly into the paths of domestic happiness.

† This rule is, as it should be, in direct hostility to a leading doctrine of Walker, who contends that *opposites* unite, whatever may be the ground of preferment or law of tastes in regard to merely *physical* qualities, which are of little account compared with those of mind and character. Phrenology recognises no such doctrine in regard to mental and moral preferences. The taste goes into this matter more deeply than the mere shape of the body, colour of the eyes or hair, &c. Both are correct. Like and unlike qualities are both essential to highest love and matrimonial bliss, as well as to endowment of offspring.

in another will agreeably excite and gratify this organ in yourself, and thus give you pleasure; but the want of moral principle in another violates your sense of right, and gives you pain, and this reversed or painful action of Conscientiousness excites your Resistance, Firmness, Intellect, Apprehension, and nearly all your other faculties *against* him.

As this principle of the reversed or painful action of the faculties bears with great force upon our conclusions, and will frequently be employed hereafter, a short digression is necessary in order to explain and illustrate it. Every faculty has both its natural and its reversed or painful action. Thus, the *natural* function of Benevolence is to feel that lively sympathy for distress which induces efforts to relieve it, whereas its reversed action is that keen anguish, that poignant grief, which the benevolent heart experiences on beholding distress which cannot be relieved. The natural function of Approbativeness is that pleasure felt when our laudable actions meet deserved commendation, but its reversed action is that shame, mortification, and chagrin caused by a consciousness of being disgraced. The natural function of Conscientiousness is that satisfaction derived from a consciousness that we have done *right*, but its reversed action produces the goadings and compunctions of a *guilty* conscience. Order is gratified by having a place for everything and everything in its place, but reversed by disorder and confusion. Size is gratified by proportion, but reversed and pained by disproportion. Ideality, in its natural action, is gratified by beholding the beautiful in nature or art, but pained and reversed by the vulgar or disgusting; and so of the other faculties. And what is more, the reversed action of any faculty calls the other faculties into reversed action. Thus, reversed Conscientiousness reverses Cautiousness, which makes the " wicked flee when no man pursueth." Reversed Self-Esteem or wounded pride, reverses Combativeness and Adhesiveness; converting the warmest friendship into the bitterest hatred; and so of other reversals.

Let us apply this principle to the reversed action of the *Social* Faculties. Though Amativeness in each sex creates a predisposition in favour of the other, yet how much greater disgust, and even hatred and abhorrence, does virtuous woman feel towards the man who has insulted her, or who would rob her of her virtue, than she can ever feel towards one of her own? No element of our nature is more powerful or inveterate than the reversed action of Amativeness and its combinations. Though Amativeness *alone* could never turn against the opposite sex, yet the *other* faculties may reverse it even against a husband or wife; the loathing and disgust, the abhorrence and *hatred* engendered thereby, can never be told. And then the lingering misery of being chained for life to a loathed and hated husband or wife, and shut out from the embraces of those that *are* loved, can be known to those only who experience it. Over such a picture let the curtains of darkness be drawn for ever !

But to return to the *reason* why we should select companions whose developments accord substantially with our own. When Ideality is large in the one and small in the other, the former will be continually disgusted and offended with the coarseness and vulgarity of the latter, and the absence of taste and gentility, of refinement, personal neatness and sense of propriety; while the latter, in turn, will be equally displeased with the former's attention to trifles, and preference of the ornamental to the useful. This disparity of tastes calls Combativeness into reversed action, and widens the breach made in their affections, till even Adhesiveness and Amativeness may become reversed, and both parties be rendered most wretched. But where Ideality is large in both, each will be continually delighted with the other's refinement of manners, delicacy of feeling, and admiration of the beautiful in nature and art; which will redouble their love, enable each to administer pleasure to the other, and thus increase their nuptial happiness. What pleases one, will gratify both, and what disgusts one, will offend both. On the other hand, when Ideality is deficient in both, each will be satisfied with home-made, common articles of dress, furniture, &c. ; the slovenliness of either, so far from offending, rather pleases, the other, and though they do not enjoy the pleasures flowing from the exercise of this faculty, yet neither of these will know their want of them.

Large Mirthfulness in the one, will throw out continual sallies of wit, which *small* Mirthfulness in the other, unable to comprehend or return, will call upon Combativeness to resent ; whereas large Mirthfulness would be gratified by such sallies, and even delight to return them.

If the husband has large Hope and deficient Cautiousness, and the wife large Cautiousness but deficient Hope, the husband, hoping everything and fearing nothing, will see only sunshine and prosperity before him, and be care- less, continually plunging into new difficulties, and be utterly incapable of sympathising with, or soothing the gloomy cast of mind which afflicts his wife, and even be displeased with it ; while she will be continually dreading the effects of his imprudence, and reproving him for it, not only without any good effect, but with his marked displeasure. She, being timid, and frightened almost at her own shadow, will feel very much in want of some careful, judicious husband, in whose care she may feel safe, yet will *be*, in fact, in the hands of an imprudent husband, who, instead of keeping her out of danger, will be continually exposing her to it, and *doubly* frightening her with both real and imaginary dangers. *He* will be continually looking upon the *bright* side of every prospect ; *she* upon the *dark* side : *he* will never see a difficulty or danger ; *she* will see more than there are, and see nothing else. How *can* they love each other? or, rather, how can they avoid mutual contention and fault-finding, and the consequent *reversal* of their social feelings ? But if each one is cautious in reference to the other, and both look at the same measures and prospects in the same light, this *similarity* of character will augment their love and increase their happiness and prosperity.

Suppose your large Benevolence fastens upon *doing good* as your chief delight, your highest duty, how can your feelings harmonise with a *selfish* companion, whose god is gain, and who turns coldly away from suffering humanity : refuses to bestow a charity, and contending with you for casting in your mite? His Selfishness *reverses* your Benevolence against him, and this not only utterly precludes congeniality in other respects, but even engen- ders that displeasure which is the very opposite of love. But if you see in our companion that same gushing fountain of humanity which overflows your own heart, how does this common feeling, this *congeniality*, swell the love and estimation of each for the other, and endear both to each other?

If thoughts of God, eternity, and things sacred be uppermost in your own mind, you can no more commingle your joys, sorrows, affections, and feelings with one who *trifles* with these things than you can assimilate oil and water, to say nothing of the painful apprehension often entertained by such that death may separate them for ever. Nor can your irreligious companion esteem or love one whom he regards as deluded or fanatical. Not only will there be a want of congeniality of views and feelings in a most important point, but your reversed religious feelings will reverse your other faculties against him, and his Combativeness be reversed against you on account of those religious feelings which you regard as most sacred, and this will be liable to reverse his love, and to root out the last vestige of affection between you. But if you both love to worship God *together*, to pray with each other, and mutually offer thanks to the " Giver of every good and perfect gift ;" if you can walk arm in arm to the sanctuary, sweetly conversing, as you go and come, upon heaven and heavenly things ; if you can mutually and cordially succour each other when tempted, and encourage each other to religious zeal, and faith, and good works, this *religious* union will unite you in other respects, and enhance your mutual esteem and reciprocal love. Unless I have seen and felt in vain, and in vain deeply pondered the volume of man's nature as unfolded in the book of Phrenology, this harmony in other respects is but the precursor—the necessary concomitant, and the co-worker of connubial love. Even when husbands and wives belong to different religious sects, this concord is essentially marred in regard both to themselves and their children.

If Approbativeness be large in the one, but small in the other, the conduct of the latter will frequently incur the reproach of his fellow-men, which will mortify and displease the other extremely, and be liable to create in each unfavourable feelings towards the other ; but if the desire for the good opinion of others be strong in *both*, each will be delighted with praises bestowed upon, and defend the character of, the *other*—be ambitious to merit the other's approbation, and so conduct themselves as to secure for both a respectable standing in society. How many men abstain from doing wrong lest they should bring disgrace upon their wives and children ? And how many more are incited to praiseworthy deeds because of the consequent honour shared with them

If the large intellectual organs of the one prefer the paths of literature to fashion, and philosophical conversation to idle chit-chat, while the weak intellectual organs and excess of vanity and Ideality of the other seek the gaudy splendour and parade of fashionable life, the former will be continually disgusted with the fashionable fooleries of the latter, and the latter equally displeased with the intellectuality of the former. But if *both* be intellectual, if both love to think and read, and especially if both prefer the same class of books and studies—which they will do if their organs are similar—they will not only be delighted to hold intellectual intercourse with each other by conversation and reading, but will be able to promote the intellectual advancement of each other ; criticise each other's ideas and productions, and continually and immensely advance each other in the main object of desire and pursuit. How exceedingly delighted must President Adams have been with the highly intellectual correspondence of his uncommonly talented wife, and how much more with the masterly manner in which she conducted the education of their son, ex-president John Quincy Adams,* and instilled into his tender mind those principles of integrity and uncompromising moral rectitude which, together with his acknowledged intellectual superiority, placed him in the presidential chair, and distinguished his long and useful life? A correspondence which is *all love* would soon cloy and sicken an intellectual companion, whilst one rich in *ideas* and good *counsel*, and also full of tenderness and elevated love, is a rare treat, a treasure which must be *experienced* to be appreciated.

If the temperament and feelings of the one be coarse and harsh, while those of the other are fine and exquisite ; if the one be phlegmatic and the other sentimental ; one quick and the other slow ; one elevated and aspiring, the other grovelling ; one clear-headed, the other dull of comprehension ; one frugal and industrious, the other idle and extravagant ; true connubial love cannot exist between them. How can *two* walk together unless they be agreed ? And if Phrenology be true, how *can* they be agreed unless their temperaments and organs be *similar?* How can husbands and wives live happily together whose tastes. dispositions, objects, sentiments, views, opinions, preferences, feelings, &c., &c., are *conflicting*, when every faculty of the one only excites those of the other to *discordant* and *disagreeable* action ; the product of which is pain, which engenders dislike? The very essence

* If any should deem this allusion irreverent or improper, let such read the published correspondence between President John Adams and his wife, *particularly* in reference to the *education of their children*, and at the same time recollect that scarcely any one thing will attach an intellectual man to his wife sooner or more effectually than to see her employ a vigorous *intellect* and an enlightened *judgment* in the training and *home* education of their children.

of connubial love, that in which alone it consists and has its being, is congeniality.

Let the reader now pause and examine the correctness of this principle. Inquire at the shrine of your own heart, and question the *experience* of the married in regard to its validity. I call upon you who are married to bear witness whether you do not love each other so far as your qualities of mind *harmonise*, and on account of that harmony. Do those of you who love and admire each other do so on account of your mental *similarity* or *dissimilarity?* And do not those of you who in part dislike each other do so because you are *unlike?* Is not the main procuring cause of that frequent want of love between husbands and wives founded in this want of *similarity of their feelings and intellectual qualities?* Does not this dissimilarity account for there being so many *pairs*, yet so few *matches?* This is *Phrenology*—this is *human nature.*

If to this you answer by asking 'how it happens that they love and marry at all since this *similarity* is the law and the basis of love, and since after marriage they find they do not possess it?' I reply that, when first 'smitten,' they find, on a casual comparison of views and feelings, that they *are* alike on some one or two strong points, and marry before they have compared notes and feelings in *other* respects. Before marriage, only the *concordant* points were brought out; after marriage their *discordant* points are brought into *collision*, and their attachments are thus *reversed.*

To every unmarried man and woman then, I say, in the name of *nature* and of nature's God, marry congenial spirits or NONE—congenial not in one or two material points, but in ALL the *leading* elements of character. And to *obtain* this congeniality, marry one whose TEMPERAMENT and PHRENOLOGICAL DEVELOPMENTS are SIMILAR TO YOUR OWN! Do this, and you are *safe*, you are *happy: fail* to do *this*, and you marry sorrow and regret.

But if this principle hold true of the *other* faculties, how much more so of the *social?* If *they* be unlike—if Amativeness or Friendship be strong in the one and weak in the other, the former will be all tenderness and affection, but the latter too cold-hearted to reciprocate them, which will put the affectionate one upon the rack. Of all other points of dissimilarity, those in regard to the *social* faculties are the *most momentous*, and disagreement *here* the most DISASTROUS! See to it, therefore, those of you who have large domestic organs, that you marry one in whom they are also large, and *not pre-occupied*, or fastened on another.

In case your own excesses or defects are liable, if equally developed in a companion, to endanger your happiness, or prove injurious to your offspring, it may be best to violate this rule, by choosing a companion whose qualities are the *opposite* of your own in these injurious extremes. Thus, if your Cautiousness be deficient, you should not marry one in whom it is also small, lest your combined imprudences keep you both always in difficulty; but you should select a companion having this organ large—one who will take care of things, and stand sentinel for you *both*, warn you of approaching danger, and check your imprudences. Though these admonitions may at times annoy you, still, if you bear in mind the *good* conferred upon you by this dissimilarity, it will only tend to *increase* your love, especially as this course was pointed out by *intellect*, and required by your own good. But if Cautiousness be so excessive in you as to produce irresolution, procrastination, or cowardice, you require a companion in whom it is less, who will be bold and prompt, and encourage you to action, as well as dispel your groundless fears. Their carelessness may often make you afraid, yet this evil is less than its excessive development in both. Still a full and *equal* development of it in each is altogether preferable.

If Acquisitiveness be small in yourself, you should by no means marry one in whom this organ is also small, lest the combined extravagance of both, and the economy of neither, bring you to poverty, and keep you there; but you should choose a frugal, acquisitive, industrious companion ; one who will make a good bargain, hold on to the purse strings, save everything, and check your profuseness.   Though this parsimony may sometimes disgust you, yet, by recollecting that this very quality benefits yourself, this dissimilarity will only serve to increase your mutual esteem and affection.   And yet, unless you saw in the light of this principle, that this disagreement worked on *your own personal good* as well as theirs, and was dictated by intellect, evil consequences would almost inevitably grow out of it.   But by 'agreeing to disagree' for the sake of the common good, this opposition of qualities, instead of breaking in upon your affections, will only *strengthen* them.

But these exceptions to this rule are few, and can occur only upon the animal propensities or lower sentiments.   On no account should they ever occur in reference to the moral sentiments or intellect.   Agreement here is indispensable to true connubial love, while disagreement here is fatal to domestic happiness.   This law is imperative.   Whoever marries in violation of it must abide the consequences, and they will be found to be *terribly* severe.

If, however, your *own* animal propensities predominate, you should by no means marry one whose animal nature *also* predominates, for this will cause a perpetual strife, and continual boiling over of the animal natures of both.   Nor should you marry one whose moral sentiments predominate ; first, because their goodness will be a living, ever-present reproof to your badness, tormenting you continually (for moral purity always rebukes selfishness) ; and secondly, because your propensities will be a perpetual thorn in the side of your companion.   As well marry a chicken to a hawk, or a lamb to a wolf, as high moral sentiments to predominant animal passions.   But, say you, If I must neither marry one having the *propensities* predominant, nor one of predominant *moral sentiments*, what *shall* I do, whom *shall* I marry ?   I'll tell thee, friend : *Don't marry at all.*   Your *own good* demands this course.   The farther you keep from the marriage state, the better for yourself and all concerned.   Till you rid yourself of your selfishness—till your *moral sentiments* rule—you are neither fit to marry nor to mingle with your fellow-men at all.   Your selfishness renders you *necessarily* miserable, and also all with whom you have to do.   So have as little to do with your fellow-men as possible, both on your *own* account and on theirs.   Above all, avoid this closest of all contacts, and especially refrain from *becoming a parent*, lest you render your posterity miserable by entailing upon them that animal organisation which torments yourself.

An extremely active *Temperament* forms another exception to this rule. When both parents are extremely active and nervous, then children will be liable to precocity, and subject to a premature death.   For the same reason two persons having small chests and weak vital powers should not become parents, but should *off-set* these defects by opposite qualities in their companions on account of offspring.   The domestic felicity of parents, and indeed of the whole family, is greatly augmented or diminished by the good or bad dispositions of the children, by their life and health, their sickness or death, &c., &c.; hence this matter becomes an item of no inconsiderable consequence to be taken into account in selecting a husband or wife.

Since this subject has thus inadvertently been broached, I will just allude to the *manifest* impropriety of choosing companions who have hereditary tendencies to mental and physical diseases, such as insanity, consumption, scrofula, apoplexy, &c., and show the importance of choosing a companion who is qualified to become the parent of healthy, moral, and intelligent offspring ; although to show *what* qualities are requisite in parents *as parents,* in order to prepare them to impart to their children the most desirable physical and mental qualities dose not come within the design of this work ; it being detailed in one on " HEREDITARY DESCENT, ITS LAWS AND FACTS."

The leading principle of Phrenology in regard to marriage, together with its *reasons*, is now before the reader. But the next inquiry is, How can this harmony be *effected ?* By what *means*, and in what *way* can it be brought about ? For to know how to *obtain* this harmony is quite as important as the harmony itself. The answers of Phrenology here also are clear and directly in point, and its directions so plain that "he that runs may read." They are—

FIRST.—STUDY YOURSELF THOROUGHLY. Study both your physical organisation and your phrenological developments. Ascertain your *own* qualities, and that will tell you just what qualities you require in a companion to harmonise with them. I say, study yourself *phrenologically ;* because no other method is equally satisfactory or certain. Without a knowledge of this science your Self-esteem, if large, will magnify all your good qualities, and throw the mantle of charity over your defects ; or, the deficiency of this organ, with large Conscientiousness, will give you too low and humble an opinion of yourself, magnifying your faults and hiding from you your good qualities. Our own organisation constitutes the medium, or the *coloured glass*, through which we look at all subjects, ourselves included. If that organisation be defective, that is, if our characters be faulty, our standard of self-estimation is erroneous, and our self-knowledge proportionably deficient or defective. But in case Phrenology be true, it affords *certain* and *tangible* data for self-examination— data that *cannot be mistaken*—so that it leaves scarcely a possibility of our being deceived or mistaken in regard to our real characters, especially when we *combine* our own *consciousness* with a knowledge of our phrenological developments.

SECONDLY.—Phrenology will also tell you the true character and disposition of your intended, and thereby show wherein each is adapted to the other, or discover their want of adaptation. Modern courtship is little else than a school of deception. The time being previously appointed, the best dress is put on, the mouth put in prim and set off with artificial smiles ; the gentleman arrayed in his best broadcloth, and the lady dressed in the height of fashion, and girt in too tightly to breathe freely or appear naturally ; fine sayings, well spiced with flattery, cut and dried beforehand ; faults all hid, and virtues set in the foreground ; and everything whitewashed for the season. And, what is even worse, the night season is usually chosen ; whereas this, the most momentous and eventful business in our lives, should be transacted in open daylight, when both parties are fully themselves, and have all their faculties in vigorous exercise. One main object of courtship should be to *become acquainted*, especially with each other's *faults*, for if the parties marry they are sure to find out these bad qualities, but it will then be too late. In trying to cheat the other party by *concealing* your faults, you are only cheating *yourselves ;* for how can those love you whom you have *deceived ?* And how can you live happily together when you both find yourselves taken in by each other ? Hence you should freely disclose your *faults ;* your virtues will exhibit themselves. Besides, persons in love are quite liable enough to be blind to the faults of their sweethearts, without any attempts to keep these faults concealed. The great danger—the *main* point to be guarded against— is a *relapse*, a *re-action after* marriage ; which will be effectually prevented by *both disclosing their faults before* marriage.

But even in case your intended should follow this almost universal custom of practising deception, a knowledge of Phrenology, with one scrutinising glance, strips the character of all artificial deceptions that can be thrown around it, and furnishes an unerring index of character, talents, tastes, sentiments, predispositions, &c.; for the *developments* can neither be inflated nor depressed to suit the occasion, but are *fixed* and *permanent* signs of the *naked character*, just as it will be found to be on acquaintance. This science, therefore, is an *invaluable* directory to candidates for marriage. If it were studied

and applied there would be no more need of making a bad choice, or of mistaking a poor husband or wife for a good one, than of mistaking a thistle for
a rose.

But if you have not sufficient time to study the science so as to apply it
with the requisite certainty for yourself, you can employ the services of an
experienced practical Phrenologist, or, if this cannot be done, a comparison of
charts, carefully prepared by him, may answer. At this course you may smile
in ridicule ; but what is there in it at all absurd, or even improper ? Is it
improper to *ascertain* the qualities of each other ? Certainly not ; whereas it
is ridiculous to marry a *stranger*, or even one of whose qualities you know but
little. Does this absurdity then consist in the proposed means of obtaining
this knowledge ? In what else can it consist ? The only reason for smiling at
this proposed method is that it is *novel*, which evinces the folly, not of this
method, but of the *laugher*. Let such laugh on, for they laugh only at themselves ; but let those who would avail themselves of an assistant superior to
all others *observe the heads* of their intended, and marry *phrenologically*. And
let matrimony, instead of being treated lightly, and as a matter of merriment,
which is usually the case, be regarded as it really is—the most momentous
business of our lives.

If to this it be objected that Cupid is blind, and that, though I have told
how to select a suitable companion, I have not shown how to *get in love* with
the one selected, I reply—

FIRST, RECTIFY YOUR STANDARD OF ESTEEM AND ADMIRATION.

If Cupid has always been blind, he has always *blindly followed admiration.*
We fall in love with whatever we admire and esteem, and with *that only.* The
young man who admires a delicate hand or handsome figure, a pretty foot and
ankle, or a fine set of teeth, a small waist or fine bust, a beautiful face, or genteel manners, mostly will fall in love with one possessing the admired quality,
and *because* she possesses it. But he who admires moral purity, or superior
talents, or piety, or tenderness of love, will love a woman possessing these
qualities, and on *account* of this quality. Is not this proposition founded in a
law of mind ? Who can controvert or essentially modify it ? To you whose
experience enables you to judge *feelingly* in regard to this matter I make my
appeal for its correctness.

This point being established, it follows that whoever regards particular
forms of the head, or certain phrenological developments, as indications of
those qualities of mind admired, will fall in love with one having these
developments just as deeply and effectually as with one having a pretty face,
handsome figure, &c., when *they* are admired, and for precisely the same reason
—namely, *because* they are admired. Why should this not be the case ? My
position, that love follows admiration, embodies the entire experience of mankind, and is invulnerable ; and the consequent inference that those who
admire an excellent head will surely fall in love with it is conclusive. Whatever, therefore, a young man or woman admires most, whether personal beauty,
a sweet smile, a talent for music, or poetry, or painting, or high intellectual or
moral attainments, or kindness, or industry, or frugality or wit, or strong
common sense, or a well-formed head, as indicating a superior mind or excellent feelings, will be fallen in love with first. To this rule there can be no
exception. By applying it you can guide your love in any channel pointed out
by intellect or sanctioned by the moral sentiments. This principle is to your
love what the helm is to a ship, and intellect should be the pilot. Let your
intellect and higher sentiments rectify your standard of admiration and
esteem, and this will effectually govern your love, and guide it into the
peaceful haven of connubial bliss.   •

Allow me to add that my own experience accords entirely with this principle, besides fully confirming the preceding, namely, that of selecting a companion by the *developments*. I say, with *emphasis*, and from *experience*, that I would place more confidence in a good phrenological head, in connection with a good physical organisation and training, than in ten years' acquaintance and courtship added to all the recommendations that can be produced. They never vary, never deceive ! while the latter may be only outside appearances. How often have they deceived the most cautious ? So often—so egregiously— that choosing a companion has been appropriately compared to buying a ticket in a lottery. You may draw a prize, but the chances are ten to one that you will draw a blank. In hundreds of instances have I seen the course here proposed of courting and marrying by the developments followed, and in as many instances have been called on professionally to decide on the fitness and the adaptation of the parties to each other, and never saw *one* to terminate otherwise than *happily*. I stake my reputation as a Phrenologist on the success of this direction properly applied, and am entirely willing to abide any evil consequences resulting from its failure.

But, continues our objector, though you show us how to make our choice, and then how to get in love with the object chosen, yet it is quite as important that you show us how to get the object of our choice in love with us. I reply, that in case the affections of the other party are not previously engaged, very little difficulty need be apprehended about engaging them ; for both young men and young women are apt to get in love quite easy enough without effort. In fact, the great difficulty consists in keeping them from loving till they are fully matured and prepared for marriage.

And now, good reader, let us pause and review the ground already gone over. The three points thus presented are—

1. THE POWER OF THE DOMESTIC FACULTIES OVER THE HAPPINESS OR MISERY OF MANKIND.

2. THE NECESSITY OF HAVING A COMPANION SIMILAR TO YOURSELF.

3. THE NECESSITY OF RECTIFYING YOUR STANDARD OF ESTEEM AND ADMIRA- TION, thus enabling you to control your love.

If this last direction should evoke the question, " By what model shall we rectify our standard ? On what principles shall this esteem and admiration be based ?" I answer, on

A FULL DEVELOPMENT OF THE MORAL SENTIMENTS.

This, according to Phrenology, is one main condition of virtue and happiness. Not only does their proper exercise give a great amount of enjoyment of the purest, highest kind, but the action of the other faculties can be productive of their proper amount of pleasure only when exercised in harmony with them, and under their sanction. The exercise of the animal propensities without their sanction, or in opposition to their dictates, is a violation of God's law, and brings down penalties on the head of the offender. By the still small voice of these sentiments man instinctively *feels* that he should be governed. He is intuitively conscious of his obligation to yield obedience to their mandates. He feels their dictates to be imperious and sovereign. When large Acquisitiveness would fain take what belongs to another, Conscientiousness, even though less in size, resists the enticement with more energy and success than Acquisitiveness urges it. It is only after the moral sentiments have been disarmed of their power by having been perverted that they allow the propensities to lead astray. No exercise of these propensities without their sanction, or at least in *opposition* to their sanction, can ultimately produce happiness, but always pain. It is a law of our nature that selfishness and sin—only another name for the predominance of the propensities—shall invariably punish themselves; and, on the other hand, that virtue and moral purity—only other names for the ascendancy of the moral sentiments properly directed—shall make their possessor happy. To enjoy the domestic relations, your moral faculties must first be exercised and gratified; and, in order to this, you require their proper development in your companion, so that this companion may continually and agreeably excite your moral faculties. If, therefore, you do not wish to be put in perpetual torment, by having your own propensities continually excited by their predominance in your companion, or if you would inhale, day by day, and year by year, the balmy breezes of high moral sentiments, of pure and holy emotion, see to it, I beseech you, that you choose a companion having large moral organs, so that your own may be continually and agreeably excited.

To *woman* this principle applies with double force: first, because she is much more under the power and subject to the caprice of her husband than he is to hers, and therefore her happiness depends more on *his* being a good-feeling man, than his happiness depends on *her* good feelings; but what is more, man is less likely to be moral and virtuous than woman; that is, woman has generally better moral developments than man, and, secondly, woman is more social, affectionate, and domestic than man; that is, she enjoys a good husband and suffers from a bad one more than it is possible for a man to enjoy a good wife or suffer from a bad one.

The reader hardly requires to be told that a predominance of the moral sentiments is indicated by a high head, and one that is long, especially on the top; while a large neck, and a thick, broad, conical head, one that runs up as it were towards a peak upon the top, somewhat resembling a cone, largest at the base, and neither high nor long, indicates the ascendancy of the propensities. Do not marry a man with a low, wide, flat head; for, however fascinating, genteel, polite, tender, plausible, or winning he may be, you will repent the day of your espousal. I would not have you marry a head too long, or too thin, lest your husband should lack the requisite force of mind and energy of character to support yourself and children; but marry a well-proportioned head and body. In my work on Education I have shown that, other things being equal, the best heads are those in which the organs are the most evenly and harmoniously developed and balanced—a principle which should be borne in mind in selecting companions for life; for, the better their characters, the greater the enjoyment you will derive from their society and affection, and, education and other things being right, the more equally developed their organs, the more perfect will be their characters, and the greater amount of brain in your head that will be called into action by them, and, consequently, the greater your happiness.

Let us now look at a few illustrations and applications of our second leading principle, namely, the importance of marrying so as to gratify the whole brain, or the moral and intellectual faculties in conjunction with the propensities, rather than to gratify the propensities merely. If your standard of admiration be beauty, and you love and marry this quality, you gratify Amativeness only, combined perhaps with Ideality and Form, so that but a small portion of your brain is exercised or gratified, nor that too long, for beauty soon fades.

So, if you admire a singing-bird, and love and marry her because she gratifies your organ of Tune, combined with one or two others, the cares of a family, blended with another kind of music, are liable to drown the tones of the piano or harp, and compel you to exclaim with Micah, "You have taken away my gods! What have I more?"

If Acquisitiveness determine your choice, and you love and marry for riches, though you may gratify a single faculty, and that a lower propensity, still you thereby violate the main law already presented, which requires the ascendancy and dictation of the moral sentiments. And you incur its penalties. Married gold generally vanishes; but even if it remain, the other party cannot fail soon to discover your motive for marrying, so that this very money is likely to become a bone of contention between you for life. No! you cannot violate this law without incurring its penalties, and these penalties are terribly severe.

The rage of American gentlemen seems to be for rich wives and small waists—both curses to any man. The habits of women brought up in affluence are anything but those calculated to make a husband happy. They usually know little or nothing of domestic matters; are neither able nor willing to work; and, worst of all, are fashionable, and fashionable life is one continued round of deception—a tissue of hollow-hearted pretensions. Rarely have such women much sterling sense, much energy of character, or much power of intellect. They expect all around them to be their waiters. They must have their every whim gratified, and all their requisitions implicitly obeyed. And then, too, most of them have been in love beforehand, and many of them several times over. The parties they have attended and the company they have seen have brought with them love scenes and disappointments, till their elements of love have been seared and blighted. And as we have hinted before, those who marry for wealth do not often secure to themselves that very wealth for which they marry, for rich girls, besides being generally destitute of both industry and economy, are frequently extravagant in their expenditure. They generally have insatiable wants, yet think that they deserve to be indulged in everything, because they placed their husbands under obligation to them by bringing them a dowry. And then the mere idea of living on the money of a wife, and of being supported by her, is too much for a man of an independent spirit. What spirited husband would not rather prefer to support both himself and wife than submit to this perpetual bondage of obligation? To live upon a father, or take a patrimony from him, is bad enough; but to run in debt to a *wife*, or to owe her a living, is too aggravating for endurance, especially if there be not perfect cordiality between the two, which cannot be looked for in money matches. Whoever violates the sacred relations of matrimony by marrying mainly for riches is accursed. He deserves to drink deep, and to drink through life, of the cup of matrimonial bitterness.*

Still I would not have you marry a companion from the depths of poverty, for extremes either way are unfavourable. The prayer of Auger, " Give me neither poverty nor riches," is the golden medium in this respect.

And to you, young ladies, let me say, with great emphasis, that those who court and marry you because you are rich will make you rue the day of your espousals. When they get your *money* they will neglect or abuse *you*, and probably squander the money itself, leaving you destitute, and abandoning you to your fate.

Do not marry an idle girl. Ladies take too much pride in cultivating delicacy and softness; refusing to labour, lest they should spoil their hands. But if working spoils their *hands*, its absence spoils their *brain;* for labour, or at least a degree of exercise, is indispensable to vigour and strength of body, and this to a vigorous brain and strong mind. Marry a working, industrious young lady, whose constitution is strong, flesh solid, and health unimpaired

---

* "What!" you exclaim, "should the rich *never* marry?" It is not against riches as such that I exclaim, but against those things that usually *accompany* them. I have elsewhere shown that the possession of great wealth violates a law of man's constitution, and therefore brings its punishment along with it. These punishments are inseparable from wealth, and therefore follow it into married life as well as everywhere else. Wherever riches go they entail unhappiness; and parents who leave their children wealthy, in this very act entail a curse upon them proportionate to the amount left them above a mere competency, including the means of intellectual and moral improvement. Let *facts* be my vouchers. Do they not bear me out in this assertion? Take it whichever way you please, rich girls make poor wives; and yet they are the first selected. Shame on sordid wife-seekers, or, rather, *money*-seekers: for it is not a *wife* that they seek, but only *filthy lucre!* They violate all their other faculties simply to gratify miserly Acquisitiveness! Verily, such "have their reward."

by confinement, bad habits, or late hours. Give me a plain, home-spun *farmer's* daughter, and you may have all the rich fashionable belles of our cities and villages.

Marrying small waists is attended with consequences scarcely less disastrous than marrying rich and fashionable girls. An amply-developed chest is a sure indication of a naturally vigorous constitution, and a strong hold on life ; while small waists indicate small and feeble vital organs, a delicate constitution, sickly offspring, and a short life. Beware of them, therefore, unless you wish your hearts broken by the early death of your wife and children. Temperance ladies have wisely adopted the excellent motto, "Total abstinence, or no husbands." Let *men* adopt the equally excellent motto, "Natural waists, or no wives." Tight-lacing is gradual suicide, and almost certain infanticide, besides exciting impure feelings.*

But to return to the necessity of amply-developed moral organs in a companion and parent. A story or two from real life will illustrate and enforce this point better than all the reasonings that can be adduced.

It was in a country village, and just before tea-time on a scorching hot day, that a boy, returning tired and hungry from the blackberry-field, entered the store of a very pious member of a church, and asked how much he would give for the berries. 'A sixpence,' answered the man of prayer, though his practised eye saw that they were amply worth double that sum. On turning them out the poor boy saw that he had not obtained half their value, and began to cry, for his heart was set upon this money to procure a much-desired gratification. 'A bargain is a bargain,' said the praying man of little conscience, as he ordered the berries to be prepared for the supper-table. 'Do let the boy have his berries or their full value,' said his conscientious and benevolent wife. This occasioned an altercation, which ended in his wife's crying along with the boy, and refusing to partake of the berries, and even of her supper. How could she relish a repast the purchase of which outraged her Conscientiousness and Benevolence, as well as exposed her husband's utter want of moral principle and good feeling ? But if Conscientiousness and Benevolence had been large in him also—if, when he saw that the sobbing boy repented of his bargain, and had not been paid enough for his berries, she had seen him pay the boy the full value of his earnings, instead of swindling him, she would have admired the noble act, loved her husband the better for his staunch integrity, and eaten the berries with a relish. But how could she love a cheat ?†

Another wife, of great kindness and a nice sense of justice, saw her husband wrong her mother, and prove ungrateful as well as untrue to his promise, and declared that for ever after this she loathed and even hated him.

Another wife caught her husband in a trifling deception, unimportant in itself, and not calculated to injure anyone, but it threw her into such an agony of feeling that the cold drops of perspiration covered her face, the colour fled from her cheeks, hope departed from her soul, and she became almost deranged ; nor is the impression effaced to this day, though she never saw a

---

* The *object* of the ladies in thus padding some parts and compressing others is to make themselves more *handsome ;* though corsets *destroy* the very beauty they are designed to impart ; for beauty depends upon *health,* and tight-lacing *impairs* health, besides shortening the period of youth. Better far adopt the Chinese method of lacing the feet, or even the flat-headed Indian method of compressing the head ; for the compression of no other part is so detrimental as that of the waist, because it retards the action of the *vital organs,* which sustain life. Abundance of exercise and fresh air is the best recipe for promoting beauty. Those who keep up the tone and vigour of their physical organs will be sprightly and interesting, and even though coarse-featured, their freshness, their wide-awake appearance, and the animated glow of their cheeks, will make a far deeper impression than laced but sickly beauty.

For a full exposition of the evils of this practice the reader is respectfully referred to my work on this subject.

† The sequel of this story is that the next January this praying cheat was imprisoned for stealing. The wife's grief on the occasion of the berries was trifling compared with that on his being imprisoned ; yet such a result might have been almost predicted ; for the man who will cheat a boy out of a cent, will cheat his fellow-men in larger matters.

similar instance after. This single trifling deception reversed her Conscientiousness, and came near reversing her devoted love for him.

Reader, suppose you bury your face in your hands, and think over similar occurrences between husbands and wives which have fallen under your own observation, and then ask yourself if all the gods in Christendom would tempt you to be similarly situated? And if you ask how to avoid such a fate, I answer, marry a companion having amply-developed moral organs.

These remarks have incidentally evolved another principle, which accounts for a phenomenon of frequent occurrence, namely, the fact that some husbands and wives can neither live together nor apart. Their organs of Adhesiveness makes them love each too well to be happy when separated; yet, some of their other faculties having become reversed, repel a close contact, and forbid their living together. They love and yet hate each other, and are in a dilemma, either horn of which is most painful, yet both might have been avoided by marrying one of kindred developments.

Other facts and illustrations on this subject might be added; but these are sufficient.

Without the strictest fidelity of each party to the other—without unreserved candour and perfect good faith—reciprocal love cannot exist, for that esteem will be destroyed on which, as already shown, true love can alone be founded.

A similar train of remark applies to marrying an economist or a worker. Each is excellent in its place, though subordinate to the character as a whole. Many men, especially in choosing a second wife, are governed by her known qualifications as a *housekeeper* mainly, and marry industry and economy. Though these traits of character are good, yet a good housekeeper is far from being a good wife. A good housekeeper may indeed prepare you a good dinner, and keep her house and children neat and tidy, yet this is but a *part* of the office of a wife. Besides all her household duties, she has those of a higher order to perform. She should soothe you with her sympathies, divert your troubled mind by her smiles and caresses, and make the whole family happy by the gentleness of her manners and the native goodness of her heart.

BEING A GOOD WIFE IMPLIES BEING A GOOD HOUSEKEEPER.

Far be it from me to underrate a good housekeeper as a constituent part of a good wife. I *know* her value, and I tell every young man that he cannot have a good wife *without* her being a good housekeeper; and I tell you, young ladies, that to be good wives you must be good housekeepers. True, this is but one duty, but it is a most important one. You cannot love a husband without wishing to make him happy, and to do this you must know how to economise; how to make his hard-earned money go as far as possible, and procure as many of the comforts of life with it as can well be obtained; how to prepare his meals properly, and gratify his appetite; how to make his home agreeable, and feed and clothe his children; how to make and mend things promotive of his comfort; and how to wait on him; for there is a certain mysterious something in the relations subsisting between husbands and wives, which renders the meal prepared by a loving wife far more palatable than the same meal prepared by a servant; an agreeable beverage still more agreeable by its being served by her; and even a bitter medicine less bitter when administered by her. For the correctness of this remark, I appeal to every man who has a good cook and housekeeper in the person of his wife. To all young men in search of a good wife, let me say, let the woman of your choice be familiar with the kitchen and the smoothing-iron. If to these she adds those graces and accomplishments requisite to shine in the parlour, so much the better; but at all events select a good housekeeper. I despise the modern notion that a wife must be too pretty and too accomplished to work. As soon would I deem it a recommendation in a woman not to know how to eat or sleep. What ! a woman look for a husband, when she does not know how to make bread or wash dishes !

Every girl should be taught to sew, spin, weave, make dresses, &c., as well as to sweep, wash, cook, &c.   Before you make an offer, see what kind of *bread* your intended can make ; for I assure you that home-made bread is better and cheaper than baker's bread.   To young men who are poor, and even to those in moderate circumstances, the qualifications on which we are insisting are invaluable, and even indispensable ; and to the rich, especially in these times of pecuniary embarrassment and uncertainty, they are scarcely less so.

And let the ladies, before giving their assent, see to it that their would-be husbands have some occupation which can be relied upon to support a family. Industry and economy are invaluable in a husband.   The man who is without them may *possibly* make a good one, yet he must have virtues many and rare to make up for these deficiencies.   Shun the dandy ; dismiss the young man of leisure who has drawn his support from a father's pocket.   If he can *love* you (which is doubtful), he cannot *support* you, and therefore, at the farthest, cannot be more than half a husband, just as you can be only a part of a wife if you do not understand domestic matters.   Get a *whole* wife or husband, or *none ;* for, while you require congeniality of feeling as the foundation, you also require these household excellencies as no inconsiderable parts of the super-structure.

A GOOD PHYSICAL ORGANIZATION AND A STRONG CONSTITUTION.

Another leading element in this standard of admiration should be a good *physical* organization, or a strong, healthy constitution.   On the importance of *health* in a companion and parent it is hardly necessary to dwell.   Many of the pains experienced by mothers as mothers have their origin in feeble constitutions or physical debility, and indicate sickly, peevish, scrofulous, consumptive, short lived children, or their pains while alive, and their premature death, to the feeble, broken constitutions of their parents.   And, what is more, the state of the mind takes its origin from that of the body.   Hence those who are subject to dyspepsia, liver complaint, indigestion, *ennui,* a sour stomach, heartburn, hypocondria, &c., &c.—which are all only different forms of the same disease, namely, the morbid excitement or predominance of the brain and nervous system—and continually oppressed with sad, melancholy feelings ; with that depression of spirits which turns everything into occasions of trouble, and sees impending misfortune in every trifling event.   It renders them miserable, and goes far towards making all connected with them unhappy.   How much more enjoyment can be taken in the company of a husband or wife who always has a cheerful and happy flow of spirits ; who requires little nursing ; who is generally healthy and able to endure fatigue and exposure, and to take a rural ramble, or turn off a smart day's work ; who does not sink under misfortune, and is not the creature of morbid feeling, &c., than in the company of a companion who is misanthropic, irritable, weakly, and often requires the doctor, or continually excites your sympathy !

Nearly all the ladies' fashions of the present day are calculated to destroy the health and ruin the constitutions of ladies, so that they must be patched up, though injured ultimately, by tea, coffee, and those other nostrums employed by invalid ladies.   Let the medical profession, and especially the vendors of quack medicines, but speak out on the subject and they will astonish all.   I refer to females, not because their health is more important, or their debility more disastrous, but because they are generally the greatest sufferers.   Behold their pale and sickly forms ; extreme delicacy and frailness ; their deficient vital organs ; their excessive nervousness ; their small waists, and slim, feeble muscles ; their sufferings as mothers, and their mental and physical debility ! And all caused by their ignorantly or fashionably violating the laws of Physiology. Even girls must be shut up in-doors and laced tight, and never be allowed to romp, because it is so ungenteel. No ! she must be a lady. Shame on such mothers ! Shame on such ladies ! Let girls romp, and let them range hill and dale in search of flowers, berries, or any other object of amusement or attraction : let them bathe often, skip the rope, and take a smart ride on horseback ; often interspersing these amusements with a turn of sweeping or washing. They will thus develop their vital organs, and lay a substantial physical foundation for becoming good wives and mothers. The wildest romps usually make the best wives ; while quiet, still, demure, sedate, and sedentary girls are hardly worth having.

Confinement often induces gloomy feeling, if not peevishness, which may usually be dispelled by a smart walk or ride, or any similar recreation. Many wives suffer extremely from debility and bad feelings, induced by excessive care and labour, and by seldom taking that recreation which is so indispensable to mental health and happiness.

Many husbands could not more effectually promote their own happiness, or the happiness of their companions, than by diverting them by means of a ride, sail, ramble, a visit to the Museum, passing an afternoon or evening with a friend, spending an hour in cultivating the garden, &c. To every husband I say, 'TAKE SPECIAL CARE OF THE HEALTH OF YOUR WIFE'—it is an invaluable treasure.

In concluding the directions for choosing a companion, I say marry so as to gratify, not *one* faculty, nor a *few* faculties, but ALL ; for it is the harmonious exercise and gratification of all which secures the height of human enjoyment. But if you cannot do this in its full extent, which might, perhaps, be too sweet a cup for erring mortals to drink, gratify as many as possible. If you are prevented from attaining the acme of human bliss, ascend as high as you can. Let no one quality of body or mind, however desirable, determine your choice ; but examine the character as a whole. And bear in mind the fact that our tastes vary much between youth and mature age. In the former period the animal feelings are much more vigorous than in after life, yet by far the greatest and best portion of life is that passed after the propensities begin to wane. Let those youth, therefore, in whom Amativeness especially is strong and ardent, or who seek to marry for *personal beauty*, remember that this ground of preference is not to continue always. And let them cater, not for their animal natures mainly, but for their moral and intellectual faculties, whose fountains of happiness never dry up, and whose streams of pleasure are always rich, and pure, and abundant.

HINTS IN REFERENCE TO CONDUCTING COURTSHIP.

To make a good selection is by no means the only important point connected with getting married. The proper method of conducting the courtship is also important. In forming the matrimonial relations let special care be taken properly to blend the qualities and assimilate the affections of each with those of the other. Not only should the faculties be similar in point of size, but, from the first, should be trained so as to act in unison and harmony with those of the other. Every unpleasant feeling during courtship is sure to have its bitter taste through life. How often do petty feelings of pride, proceeding from the jealousy, or distrust, or guilty conscience of the complaining party, construe a fancied neglect or imaginary provocation, wholly undesigned by the other, into occasions of disaffection, which frequently widen into reciprocal coldness, if not into mutual accusations, and thereby break off, at least for a time, their growing attachments, leaving both most wretched. Each loves the other, and yet, while their affections incline them one way, their pride or Combativeness drives them the other. This *clashing* of the faculties is the most unhappy state of mind imaginable. Beware how you set your faculties at war with each other. Why make yourself miserable merely to tease and torment the object of your affections? Recollect your liability to become jealous without cause in consequence of the principle before explained, and, therefore, make abundant allowances, as well for yourself as for your intended. Close the breach; heal the wound; make mutual concessions; and never let your pride conflict with love. And let young gentlemen especially remember that they are more liable to give occasions of offence than young ladies; for it is almost impossible for a woman who is in love to ill-treat the object of her love. Then again, young ladies suffer more from these interruptions of affection than young men, because their attachments are so much stronger and more tender, and they have so much less to divert their minds from the cause of their grief. Follow the advice already given, in first choosing *intellectually*, and then let no petty feeling of pride or anger interrupt your love. Give no occasion of offence, and be slow to receive one. The acknowledged principle that we dislike those we have injured shows that those who are angry first, or most, are usually the most in fault.

THE AGE MOST SUITABLE FOR MARRYING.

On this point a great diversity of opinion exists. The number of years is not material. The vigour and youthfulness of the constitution are most important. Some are older at twenty than others at twenty-five. Never ask how many years old one is, but only how much animal and mental vigour, or how much youthfulness and ardour there is. A broken constitution begins to decline at seventeen, while a strong, unimpaired constitution is in its prime at forty. These remarks apply both to the absolute age suitable for marrying and to the comparative ages of the two parties. I incline to the opinion that between twenty and thirty is the age designed by nature, and the one most suitable *in itself*; yet persons from short-lived families mature much earlier, and are inclined to marry much younger than those from long-lived families. Those who are inclined to marry very young are generally prematurely developed, and often die early. Exceptions occur, yet this principle forms a law of our being.

Franklin, in a letter to a newly-married friend, advocated early marriage, on the ground that *nature* would indicate the most suitable time by imparting the requisite feelings or instinct. In this he was *philosophically* right, but *practically* wrong, as will appear on referring to those causes which develop Amativeness prematurely. Let nature have her perfect work, and she will then indicate the proper time by implanting the requisite feelings; but that artificial state of society in which we live violates her laws, and causes her to lead men wofully astray in this respect. One thing is certain, that, at all events, marriage should be postponed till the growth is completed, the physical organisation well nigh consolidated, the judgment matured, and till both parties have obtained a tolerably good practical knowledge of physiology as well as of the best method of nursing and educating children.

arly marriages have one important advantage—that of the more easily assimilating the feelings and adapting the habits to each other; but they have the disadvantage of a judgment too immature to select the best object of affection; while late marriages have a disadvantage of far greater magnitude, that of marrying a second or twentieth love, which is well nigh sufficient, as we shall presently see, for ever to blast true connubial love. As society now is, it is my unequivocal opinion that early marriages, say from *fifteen to twenty*, are the best, if not almost indispensable to virtue and connubial happiness.*

---

* This is said in reference to Americans. From twenty to twenty-four may be the best time for people in England. The Americans are men and women a few years earlier than the English.

Of the two evils, of marrying without judgment, or of marrying *with* judgment but *without love,* choose the former, for it is the least. But a more conclusive reason for this opinion will be given under a subsequent head.

AN IMPROPER OBJECTION TO EARLY MARRIAGES.

Many mothers object to their daughters marrying young, on the ground that married women not only take little or no enjoyment, but are rendered unhappy by the cares of the family, and by being shut out from all the pleasures of society. What an idea this! What a reflection on this heaven-born institution! Those whom marriage renders unhappy, or even those whose pleasures it abridges, had better not marry at all.

But what is the origin of this blasphemous idea? Why, that all the pleasures of young ladies are summed up in attending balls, parties, sleigh-rides, pleasure excursions, love-scrapes, courting, flirting with the beaux, to secure a more advantageous match, and things of this class! It certainly can have no other origin. It is an impious reflection on the marriage institution and on the family relations. I scorn the mother who would postpone marriage an hour to allow the daughter an opportunity to take a little more *pleasure.* In so doing, people condemn marriage as an evil, and imply that matrimony is a hateful altar on which woman with all her hopes and prospects must be sacrificed—that married life is a slavish and intolerable drudgery, and therefore to be postponed as long as possible. And to these women who do postpone marriage from this wicked motive, married life is all that they fear; for they marry from interest, not from love, and therefore experience all the miseries, and none of the blessings, already described. Those *mothers* who entertain so repugnant an idea of marriage, only show what kind of wives and mothers they have been. The sooner this relation is entered into, after the intellect of the parties is sufficiently matured to choose the proper object, the better.

SINGLE BLESSEDNESS.

But some choose not to marry at all, but prefer a life of single blessedness. And I grant that it is better not to marry, than to marry a bad husband or wife; for it is obviously better to let the social organs remain unexercised, than to have them reversed or painfully exercised. Still marriage is just as much a part of our nature as talking or eating, and cannot therefore be dispensed with without serious detriment.*

To those whose social organs are both large and active, Phrenology says, with all the emphasis of a law of our being—MARRY! Marry *soon,* or else cease exercising your social faculties; because, besides foregoing the virtuous pleasures of that quiet, unchecked, and reciprocal exercise of the social faculties afforded by marriage, their ungratified action, or their vicious indulgence, will inevitably make you miserable.

---

* I really pity those young people, especially young ladies, whose domestic feelings are strong, whose hearts are gushing fountains overflowing with love and tenderness, but who have no fit object on which to bestow them. Who does not pity the cooing dove without its mate? Such anomalies rarely, if ever, occur in nature generally, nor should they occur in reference to man or woman. How many maiden ladies who are every way qualified to make the best of wives and mothers are doomed to live unmarried and to die unmourned! And many of this class are the very BEST of the sex—those whose feelings of love are of that exquisite character which, once disappointed, for ever afterwards refuse to violate the sacredness of their first love by a second engagement. Some of them are doubtless too particular, others too cautious, but the majority too tenderly endeared to some congenial spirit ever to cast an eye of love upon any other than him who bore off only to blight their first full-blooming affections. Let them not be ridiculed, but rather let them be commended for being thus true to nature, or rather, for having so much nature in them. And then, too, they render themselves very useful in families, neighbourhoods, and societies, as teachers, nurses, makers of garments, &c. But they should not expect to live as long or as happily as they would had they married well while young.

Phrenology, therefore, recognises and enforces this, as one of the first com mands of God : 'Be fruitful and multiply, and replenish the earth.' Become husbands, wives, and parents ; so that your social faculties may have full scope for action, together with the delightful objects for the combined exercise of the other faculties. You cannot be a whole man or woman, unless all your faculties are brought into pleasurable action upon their legitimate objects.

Many persons, particularly young men, refuse to marry, because they cannot support a wife in the style they wish. To this I reply, that a *good* wife will care less for the style in which she is supported than for *you*. She will conform to your necessities cheerfully, and be happy with you in a log cabin. She will even help you to support yourself. To support a good wife, even if she have children, is generally less expensive than to board alone, besides being one of the surest means of acquiring property. This false pride of wishing to support a wife in style, is really pernicious in its influences both on yourself and on woman. It tends to divert its entertainers from the proper motive of marriage, namely, *domestic enjoyment*.

MARRYING FOR A HOME MERELY.

Do not, however, marry for a *home* merely, unless you wish to become even more destitute with a home than without one, for it is on the same footing with "marrying for money." I know a lady who, when an orphan child, lived with a relative who abused her beyond measure, and who, at an early age, married, not because she had the least spark of affection for her husband, but to free herself from her uncle, and be independent of her friends. But, to use her own expression, "she jumped out of the frying-pan into the fire." I will not enter into particulars, but suffice it to say, that she described her situation as horrible beyond description, and that of her daughters as scarcely less so. The father, who should have loved and cherished his daughters for her sake as well as his own, hated and abused them on her account. She could not live with her husband, because his physical abuse was intolerable. She therefore obtained a divorce. Nor could she be comfortable separated from him, on account of her children ; so that her sufferings can only be ended with her life. What a wretched life would the timely perusal of this work have saved her ! "He that hath ears to hear, let him hear."

MARRY TO PLEASE NO ONE BUT YOURSELF, NOT EVEN YOUR PARENTS.

I know a lady who, to please a widowed mother and provide her a home, married a man for whom she had not a spark of love, and who, to obtain her, had artfully courted the mother rather than the daughter. Her marriage was the destruction of her pleasures, and the grave of that very mother who had persuaded her into it. Because the mother would not give him the command of a thousand dollars (it was this thousand dollars that he courted and married), the interest of which was her main support, he became her enemy, and made her life most wretched, and then exposed her in such a manner as to cause her death as effectually as if he had poisoned her.

Parents can no more *love* for their children than they can eat or sleep for them. They may give advice, but should leave the decision to the judgment of the parties themselves. Besides, such is human nature, that to *oppose* lovers, or to speak against the person beloved, only increases their desire and determination to marry. The beloved one is considered as abused, and this sympathy strengthens love and weakens the influence of those who oppose, and thereby furthers the match by preparing the way for an elopement. Many a runaway match would never have taken place but for unwise opposition. Reason with them mildly, and then throw the responsibility on them. Never disinherit, or threaten to disinherit, a child for marrying against your will. If you would make your daughter marry a man whom you do not wish her to marry, oppose her violently, and she will be almost sure to marry him ; so also with a son.

The fact is, however, that such should be the relations between parents and children, that the latter should apply to parents for advice on the first pulsation of love. Let the father properly train his daughter, and she will bring her first love-letter to him, and give him an opportunity to cherish a suitable affection, or to nip an improper one in the germ.

There is, however, one way of preventing an improper match, and that is not to allow your children to associate with any one you are unwilling they should marry. It is cruel, as well as unjust, to allow a daughter to associate with a young man till her affections are rivetted, and then forbid her to marry him. Forbid all association or consent cheerfully to the marriage.

"But," answers a purse-proud mother, "my daughter has fallen in love with our hired man ! How could I prevent them being together?" Good madam, if your hired man be immoral or unworthy, exclude him from your family ; if he be intelligent or worthy, he may be as good as your daughter, for labour is neither a dishonour nor a crime, but just the contrary. If you are still determined that your daughter shall not marry a poor man, and yet must have a young man to do your drudgery, I see no other way but for you to hire a *rich* young man to do your drudgery, or else to break your daughter's heart, and render her miserable for life.

DO NOT MARRY AN INTEMPERATE COMPANION.

So many and so aggravated are the instances of matrimonial suffering produced by marrying companions of intemperate habits, that a passing allusion to this subject is required. Intemperance is the parent of all vices. Such is the relation between the body and the base of the brain, or the animal propensities, that the stimulant afforded by alcoholic drinks excites these animal propensities, while it disables the moral sentiments, or intellect, and hence induces vice in all its forms.

Do not flatter yourself that your intended is only a moderate or an occasional drinker, for moderate drinking is the only cause of drunkenness. I never see a young lady tip a glass of wine in company without feeling troubled on her account. Wine is as bad for ladies, and for the higher or sedentary classes, as rum or brandy is for the labouring classes. To every young man, then, I say, do not marry a wife who drinks either wine or porter ; if you do, you will rue. You will, ten to one, find her irritable and peevish, and liable not to be virtuous. Every form of alcoholic drink excites Amativeness, which exposes any woman, when slightly exhilarated (I do not mean intoxicated), to be taken advantage of. If the exhilarating effects of ardent spirits render a man liable to be taken advantage of in business,* then surely the exhilaration produced by any kind of ardent spirit, even by wine, exposes a woman to be taken unawares, and robbed of her most costly jewel. No wine-drinking woman is safe, even though she drinks only enough to become slightly exhilarated, for it is the exhilaration that does the mischief. Let those young men who gallant the ladies home from balls and parties where wine is drunk be my vouchers. For a woman to drink wine, or any kind of exhilarating drinks, I deem immodest and vulgar. Only wine-drinking women will object to this, and they know it to be true.

And to every young woman I would say, adopt the motto, "Total abstinence or no husband," for there is a world of philosophy in it. Unless a young man abstain totally from every form and degree of intoxicating drinks, he is in danger, aye, almost sure to become a drunkard, and not only neglect

---

* And this is conceded on all hands ; for the most effectual way to take advantage of a man is first to treat him, not till he is drunk, but till he becomes excited and exhilarated.

to provide for a wife, but to drink up even her earnings, and abuse her in at the bargain. It is infinitely better to have *no* husband than a drunken one. I appeal to you, wives and mothers of drinking husbands, if you would not infinitely prefer never to have been married ! Are not words inadequate to describe your sorrows and your sufferings, both on your own account and on account of your children ?

Do not flatter yourselves that you can *wean* a drinker from his cups by love persuasion. Intoxicating drink at first kindles up the fires of love into the fierce flames of burning licentiousness, which burn out the very element of love, and destroy every vestige of pure affection. It over-excites Amativeness, and thereby finally destroys it, producing at first unbridled libertinism, and then an utter barrenness of love, besides reversing the other faculties of the drinker against his own consort, and those of the wife against her drinking husband. Read my work on " Intemperance," and you will never wish to marry even a moderate drinker, though it be a moderate drinker of wine only.

But another direction, more important, if possible, than any yet given is—

DO NOT ALLOW THE DOMESTIC FACULTIES TO BECOME ENGAGED UNTIL YOU HAVE MADE YOUR CHOICE AND OBTAINED CONSENT.

It has been already shown that no small part of man's happiness or misery depends upon the condition of his Social Faculties. Love is one of the most sacred elements of our nature,* and the most dangerous with which to tamper. It is a beautiful and delicately-contrived organ, producing the most delightful results, but easily thrown out of repair. The domestic faculties are generally easily injured. It is with them as with Conscientiousness, Benevolence, Approbativeness, Veneration, &c. How pungent, how overwhelming, are the first compunctions of a guilty conscience ! But every new violation wears off its tender edge, and blunts the moral sensibilities. So, when Approbativeness in a child, especially in a girl, is first wounded by reproof or reproach, her feeling of shame and mortification are so intolerable that she knows not where to hide her head. Her face is crimsoned with the blush of shame and sense of disgrace. But reproaches and blame frequently administered sear this faculty, and she now cares little for all the reproaches that can be heaped upon her. So, also, when a man whose heart is all alive to the miseries of sensitive beings sees an animal killed for the first time, or a fellow-being racked with pain, reversed Benevolence inflicts greater agony than that endured by the object pitied ; yet a number of such sights so effectually harden the heart as even to prepare him to take part himself in killing animals. His Benevolence is seared, never again, perhaps, to experience that exquisite pity which accompanied its primitive, unviolated tenderness. So with regard to Veneration, Ideality, Cautiousness, and every other faculty. This principle applies to the *social* faculties. And since these organs are very large, the evils attendant upon their violation are proportionably great.

But how are these faculties seared? By the interruption of love. Interrupted love places its sufferers in the same position, with regard to loving subsequently, that violated Conscientiousness does with regard to moral principle, or being disgraced with regard to character, or witnessing pain with regard to sympathy. To love after this interruption with the same purity and tenderness as before is perhaps impossible.

Candidates for marriage, remember this law of mind. See to it, if possible, that your love is never interrupted. Do not allow your affections to become engaged till you have made your choice, and are tolerably certain of marriage.

* What is called sudden love has its origin mainly in the action of Amativeness, and is another name for animal passion. True love is slower of growth—always mutual and reciprocal, and founded in esteem, and in an admiration of moral and intellectual qualities ; while sudden love is excited by physical charms.

Courting without intending to marry, and parental interference with their children's affections, beside causing an incalculable amount of prostitution and wretchedness, render a large portion of the marriages of the present day unhappy. Good people mourn over these evils, but seldom dream of their cause. They even pray for moral reform, yet do the very things that increase the evil. Do you see yonder godly mother weeping over her fallen son, and remonstrating with him in tones of a mother's tenderness and importunity? That very mother prevented that very son marrying the girl he dearly loved because she was poor, and this interruption of his love was the cause of his ruin. If she had allowed him to marry this beloved one he would never have thought of giving his "strength unto strange women." True, the mother ruined her son ignorantly, but none the less effectually. That son next courts another virtuous fair one, engages her affections, and ruins her, or else leaves her broken-hearted; so that she is more easily ruined by others; and thus prepares the way for her becoming an inmate of a house "whose steps take hold on hell." Meanwhile, this spuriously-godly mother prays daily for the "Magdalen cause," and gives monthly to Moral Reform Societies. She means no harm (only to have her son marry wealth and fashion), but does wickedly and ignorantly perpetrate a crime of the blackest dye. Ah, proud, but foolish mother! Oh, ruined and abandoned son! Alas, wretched victims? If the painful consequences attached to this violation of the social feelings by this courting and loving without marrying were confined to the principal offender, the evil would be less, for every voluntary agent has the privilege of doing for himself as he pleases; but he certainly has no right to plant thorns of anguish under the pillow of his wife, or, rather, of his *victim*.

I say, then, that no man should ever pay his addresses to a woman until he has made his selection. He should first make his selection intellectually, and love afterwards. He should go about the matter coolly and with judgment, as he would undertake any other important matter. No man, when blinded by love, is in a fit state to judge advantageously as to what he requires, or who is adapted to his wants. I know, indeed, that this doctrine of choosing first and loving afterwards—of excluding love from the councils, and of choosing with the consent of the intellect and moral sentiments, is often at variance with the feelings of the young and the customs of society; but, for its correctness, I appeal to common sense. This is the *only proper* method. Phrenology requires, as an indispensable condition to virtue and enjoyment, that the propensities (that of love included) should be governed by the moral sentiments and intellect; and the more momentous the matter, the more imperious this requisition. Shall we, then, in this, the most momentous and eventful transaction of our lives, be governed by blind animal feelings? Science forbids it. Your own happiness forbids it. Hold then a tight rein upon your love till intellect shall have designated a suitable time, and selected a suitable object on whom it may rest for ever, and the full fruition of all those joys designed by God to flow from marriage will abundantly reward you for this temporary self-denial.

And especially let no young lady ever once think of bestowing her affections till she is tolerably certain they will not be broken off—that is, until the match is fully agreed upon. Let her keep her heart whole till she bestows it for life. This requisition is as much more important, and its violation as much more disastrous, to woman than to man as her social faculties are stronger than his. You cannot be too careful in your love—it is the pivot on which turn your destinies for life.

But here an apparently insurmountable difficulty arises to prevent putting this direction in practice. These matrimonial instincts generally develop themselves early, long before the judgment is matured, and often rage to a degree well nigh ungovernable, refusing to wait till the tardy intellect has made its selection, and has all things ready. In such cases, what must be done? Kind reader, listen—moralists and philanthropists attend—while I strike the very root of this poisonous tree of domestic bitterness—while I lay open the cause of this unblushing licentiousness, which constitutes the sin of this sinful age—this neucleus of all the vices—this hell upon earth, whose fierce flames are continually consuming the life and souls of millions, by inflicting upon them all the mental and physical agonies which our nature can bear. That cause is the *premature development* and the *artificial stimulation* of Amativeness. I will expose a few of these causes, kept in constant operation by nearly all classes of the community, which tend to bring forward the passion of love prematurely, and to keep it constantly and morbidly excited.

1. THE IMPROPER CONDUCT AND CONVERSATION OF ADULTS BEFORE CHILDREN AND YOUTH. Nothing could more effectually wear off that natural delicacy, that maiden purity and bashfulness in youth, which form the main barrier against the influx of vitiated Amativeness, than the conduct and conversation of some who are even parents. How often do those whose modesty has been worn smooth, take pleasure in saying and doing things to raise the blush on the cheek of youth and innocence, little dreaming perhaps that they are thereby breaking down the barriers of their virtue, and prematurely kindling the fires of animal passion !

As puberty approaches the evil magnifies. The prematurely-kindled embers of love now burst forth into the flames of licentiousness or self-pollution. The machinery of balls and parties, of dances, of the other amusements of young people, tend to fan the flame. Thus they court and form attachments long before either their mental or physical powers are matured.

2. READING NOVELS, LOVE TALES, &C., &C. The fashionable reading of the day is still more objectionable. Whose sales are the greatest? Whose patronage is the most extensive? Those who publish the most exciting love tales. Country newspapers must have a part or the whole of some love tale every week, or else they are run down. These stories girls are allowed to read. How often have I seen girls not twelve years old as hungry for a love story as they would have been for their dinners. Their minds are thus sullied with impure desires. Shame on novel-reading women ; for they cannot have pure minds or unsullied feelings.

3. A STIMULATING DIET preternaturally excites and prematurely develops this organ. There is an intimate relation between the state of the body and that of the animal propensities. Whatever artificially stimulates the body stimulates the animal propensities. Tea, coffee, flesh, tobacco, spices, &c., as well as wine and ardent spirits, are highly stimulating, and therefore powerfully excite these propensities. The inference is clear that stimulating food and drink tend to develop this organ prematurely, and keep it in a morbid, feverish state of action. Children, therefore, should not be allowed a stimulating diet, nor is it exactly proper for young ladies.

4. WANT OF EXERCISE is another means of exciting impure desires ; while labour tends to subdue them. As the energies of the system are continually accumulating, they must have some door to escape. Labour and exercise carry them off through the muscles ; but when this door is closed by fashionable idleness, their next medium of egress is through the propensities. This is established by facts. What classes of society are most virtuous? The labouring. Who are the most licentious? The idlers—men and women of leisure—those who are too good to labour. When the labourer retires he falls asleep at once, while those who are too proud or fashionable to work retire to indulge the nightly reveries of their fancies, mingled with unclean thoughts and stained with impure desires. Labour is as indispensable to moral purity as breath is to life. This is a law of our being. All who break it, even

fashionable ladies included, must abide the consequences ; one of which is a depraved imagination and unclean desires.*

This principle applies with increased force to *children and youth.* Keeping them housed up indoors, from play or labour, tends to ripen Amativeness prematurely, and then to keep it morbidly active. This is the cause of its appearing two or three years earlier in the city than in the country, and several years earlier *there* than unthwarted *nature* would develop it. Were these and other causes of its premature development done away, it would not probably appear till between the twentieth and twenty-first year, and then be five years longer in ripening up to a maturity sufficient for marriage ; and by this time the judgment would be sufficiently matured to make a proper selection.

5. Theatres and theatrical dancing also inflame Amativeness, and are "the broad road" to moral impurity. Much of the fashionable music is another, especially the *verses* set to it, being most love-sick ditties, or sentimental odes, breathing this passion. Improper prints often do immense injury in this respect.

6. But nothing perhaps tends to develop or inflame this passion so much as *modern female education.* It seems as though the one main object of the education of fashionable females was to excite and gratify the Amativeness of fashionable gentlemen, to enable them to get a dashing beau and a rich husband. Most of our fashionable boarding-schools are public curses. These schools teach the *graces* and *accomplishments* mainly, which are only polite names for beau-catching, cap-setting, and such like fashionable attainments. They efface almost every element of the true woman. They teach her to screw her waist into artificial forms, and her face into artificial smiles, and to learn to say soft things very softly. They inculcate in effect the sentiment that the chief end of woman is to please the men, and pander to their depraved appetites ; that to engage personally in domestic duties is a violation of good breeding and even downright vulgarity ; that a lady must know how to draw, embroider, sing, write letters ; that dress, and show, and fashion, and splendid style must supersede all other considerations ; that extravagance is a virtue, and economy meanness : that making morning calls and fashionable parties, and telling polite lies (that is, pretending to be very glad to see persons whom they dislike, and pressing them to call again, when they hate the very sight of them), together with a thorough knowledge of the art of making love and playing the coquette, and such like fashionable flummery, constitute the main duty of woman. A recent English work devoted to teaching ladies *manners,* occupied some fifteen pages in teaching them how to get into a carriage, so as to show just enough, but none too much, of their handsome ancles, feet, &c., &c. If there be any one thing in civilised society more utterly destitute of common sense, and evincing more consummate folly, or if there be anything more totally at war with the designs and arrangements of nature than any other, it is the modern fashionable method of conducting female education.

In view of these evils, one gentleman of this city said—" I would sooner let my daughter run wild, than receive a modern fashionable education ; " and another observed, " Though I would not go to that extent, yet I would sooner see my daughters get their living by *begging,* or follow them to their graves to-morrow, than brought up fashionably." Over no evil do I mourn more— no crime do I deplore more—than the perversion of woman's nature by modern education.† I call upon woman to pause, and consider the oppressive evils

---

* Every labourer will bear me witness that these feelings are more active when they do *not* work than when they do.

† As soon as I can command the time, I intend to publish, in a neat little book, a LADIES EDITION of this work, which, besides being free from all expressions and allusions to which even prudish fastidiousness can object, will be expressly adapted to *woman* in the matter of marriage and education, showing her how she should be educated to become a wife and matron, and then how to choose and obtain a suitable husband.

under which she groans, and to rise and shake off her chains, and follow the
dictates of her nature ; to assert and maintain her independence ; to rise from
her abject servitude ; * to assert and maintain her rights and her freedom
and be herself.

MARRY YOUR FIRST LOVE.†

I have before stated that interruptions in love *sear* and *benumb* the element
of love.   I do not say you cannot love a second time ; but I do say that first
love experiences a tenderness, an exquisiteness, and a poetry not always
belonging to subsequent attachments.

MUTUAL LOVE CONSTITUTES MATRIMONY.

How absurd, how preposterous, the doctrine that the obligations of marriage derive their sacredness from legal enactments.   How it profanes this
holy of holies.   Marriage is wholly divine both in its origin and obligations.
No human tribunal or legislature can increase or diminish those obligations.

The happy, loving pair are always married in heaven before they are on
earth ; for their agreement to live together in nature's holy wedlock is
marriage in the sight of God, and constitutes them husband and wife.   Still,
since a ceremony has been instituted, it may be well to observe it as a form,
if we can do it conscientiously.

The perpetuity of love's nature has provided for, and infinitely better than
man can do ; and therefore man need not feel concerned about it.   Let men
rely on the affections of the heart alone, for their very nature is self-perpetua-
ting.   They need no law, and are above all law.   Let them be properly
placed at first, and they will never desire to change their object.   The more
we love an object, the more we wish to continue loving it ; and the longer
husbands and wives live together affectionately, the stronger their love.
Love increases itself.   We no more need a law requiring husbands and wives
to love each other than one requiring us to eat, sleep, or breathe.   True love
recoils from a change of objects.   Let men but rely upon the law of love
instead of upon the laws of the land, and they will have far more connubial
happiness, and the country would hear of far fewer discords and petitions for
divorce.   Nor should the law ever compel two to live together who do not
love each other.   At the same time, the laws respecting marriage are cruelly
oppressive, especially upon *woman*, whom they ought to protect.

The inference, therefore, is clear, that those whose legal marriage is
prompted by motives of property, or honour, or any consideration other than
mutual love, are no more husbands and wives than if they had never assented
to the marriage ceremony.   Does their nominally assenting to a mere man-
made ceremony make them husbands and wives ?   It simply legalises prostitution.   It is licensed licentiousness.   If they do not love each other, they
cannot become husbands and wives, or be entitled to the sacred relations of
wedlock.

So, on the other hand, if two kindred spirits are really united in the bonds
of true, reciprocal love, whether legally married or not, they are to all intents
and purposes man and wife, and entitled to all the rights of wedlock.   If
they have reciprocated the pledge of love, and agreed to live together as

---

* For years, the fact that Self-esteem is small in nearly all women, and Firmness rather feeble,
surprised me ; but Phrenology soon opened my eyes to the true situation of woman—that of
abject *slavery* to a dozen masters— to the fashions, which make her pinch her feet and screw in
her waist till she can have no peace of her life ; a slave to man, especially the worst class of men
—the genteel class ; and a slave to the artificial wants of man, in the family and out of it ; a slave
in almost every form in which it is possible for a man to command or woman to obey.

† First love, as employed here and elsewhere in this work, refers to the first strong, reciprocal
attachment, founded in esteem, and formed after the parties arrive at an age sufficient to
experience the full power of love.

man and wife, they are married. They have nothing to do with law, or law
with them, except so far as they may consider it expedient. It is a matter
exclusively their own. And for proud and selfish parents, from motives of
property or family distinctions, to interfere or break up the match, is as
criminal and cruel as separating husband and wife—it is separating them ; it
is a violation of the married relations ; it is *putting asunder* those whom *God*
hath joined together. Ambitious mothers, selfish fathers, and young men
seeking to marry a fortune, may stare or startle at this ; but any other view
of marriage makes it a merely human institution, which divests it of its
sacredness and dignity.

Again. For a young man to court a young woman, and excite her to love
till her affections are rivetted, and then (from sinister motives, such as to
marry one richer, or more handsome) to leave her, is the very same crime as
to divorce her. So, also, for a young woman to play the coquette, and sport
with the sincere affections of an honest and devoted young man, is one of the
highest crimes that human nature can commit.

Young men and women, let these things sink deep into your hearts !
Pause and reflect ! and, in every step you take towards loving and marrying,
remember that mutual love constitutes matrimony ; and that interrupting
love is separating man and wife !

SECOND MARRIAGES.

In case a companion dies, marrying again may be a less evil than living
unmarried. But I maintain that the death of a companion need not occur
till too late to marry again. The proof of this startling declaration is, first,
that every physiological law of our nature—every physical contrivance and
adaptation of the body—fully establishes the inevitable conclusion, that, in
case of the laws of life, health, and physiology were obeyed, sickness would be
unknown, and death would occur only after the body was literally worn out
with old age ; and secondly, that sickness and death are merely the effects of
their appropriate causes, and governed by fixed laws, and therefore within our
control. By applying the appropriate means (which are in the hands of
ourselves, our parents, and mankind) all may be healthy, and live to a good
old age ;* so that husbands and wives need not be separated from each other
or from their children by death until the former are too old to marry again,
and the latter old enough to provide for themselves (extraordinary cases, of
course, excepted). This renders the inference clear and most forcible, that
all men and women are under obligations the most imperious and sacred to
their families to take care of their health ; and to avoid all exposures calculated to shorten life. Their duties to their families are amongst their *first*
duties. Their obligation to preserve their health is *paramount ;* so much of
the happiness of their families depends upon their health, and the sufferings
caused by their sickness and death are so excruciating and aggravated.

It should be added, that it is the duty of parents to be at home as much
as possible, and in the bosom of their families, making them glad by their
presence, and causing them to enjoy the sweets of domestic life. They
should banish as much as possible all those unpleasant feelings engendered
by losses, impositions, vexations in business, &c., and place their domestic
feelings and higher sentiments on the throne, relaxing their souls, and even
playing with their children. How often are angry and unpleasant feelings
carried into the family to mar their joys, and how natural to pour them out
upon its innocent members, not because they have done anything wrong, but

* If this doctrine be deemed heretical or chimerical, I answer, 1st, that Charles G. Finney
advocates it ; 2ndly, that Physiology establishes it to a *demonstration ;* and 3rdly, that any other
view of this matter substitutes *chance* in the place of *cause* and *effect.* It is high time for mankind to know that sickness and death, in the prime of life, are merely the *penalties* of violated
physical laws, and therefore *wrong.*

because we were previously in anger !' When anger has been excited, how natural to direct it to those about us, though entirely innocent ; but how *unreasonable*, especially if they be an affectionate wife or innocent children.

In regard to marriage, then, the order of nature, as pointed out by Phrenology, is unquestionably this : 1st, that the matrimonial instincts or feelings should not appear till from the twentieth to the twenty-first year : 2nd, that true love requires from three to five years to ripen into a preparation for marriage : 3rd, that by this time the moral and intellectual faculties will generally have become sufficiently matured to select the proper object upon which they may fix for life in virtuous wedlock : and 4th, that then, the happy pair, hand in hand and heart in heart, should climb the hills and walk the vales of life together, commingling their joys, their sorrows, and affections, until each becomes too old to marry again ; so that both may pay the common debt of nature nearly together, loving and marrying but once ; thus combining all the intellectuality of a mature mind with all the poetry of *first love.* This is marriage in full fruition—marriage as ordained by God, and as woven into the nature of man.

DIRECTIONS TO THE MARRIED FOR LIVING TOGETHER AFFECTIONATELY AND HAPPILY, AND FOR MAKING FAMILIES HAPPY AND NEIGHBOURHOODS AGREEABLE.

1. EXCITE EACH OTHER'S FACULTIES AGREEABLY. The following principle shows how to do this :—The activity of any faculty in one naturally excites the same faculty in others. Combativeness in one, for instance, excites Combativeness in others, while Benevolence excites Benevolence, &c. Thus, when kindness in a brother does you a favour, you are anxious to return it, Benevolence in him exciting Benevolence in you ; but anger kindles your own anger, and causes in you a spirit of resistance and resentment. For example :

Mr. Sharp* said, angrily, to a lad, 'Go along, and bring me that basket yonder. Be quick, or I'll flog you !' The boy went tardily and poutingly, muttering as he went. 'Why don't you hurry there, you idle vagabond, you ? Come, be quick, or I'll whip your lazy hide off your back, you saucy, impudent rascal, you,' re-echoed Mr. Sharp, still more imperatively. The boy went still more slowly, and made up a face still more scornful, for which Mr. Sharp flogged him ; and, in return, the boy conceived and cherished eternal hatred to Mr. Sharp, and eventually sought and obtained revenge. But Mr. Benign said, kindly, to the same boy, 'John, will you please to run and bring me that basket ?' 'Yes, sir," said John, and off he started on the run, glad to do the good old man a favour.

2. ADAPT YOURSELF TO THE PHRENOLOGICAL DEVELOPMENTS OF YOUR COMPANION.

Thus, if Hope be large in the husband, but small in the wife, he magnifies every prospect, and underrates difficulties and dangers ; but she, especially if her Cautiousness be large, looks at them in a light directly opposite. She fears, and perhaps frets ; he hopes and rejoices. If Anger be large or active, each will be inclined to blame the other for this difference of views. The husband, instead of chiding his wife for her groundless fears, should *encourage* her, and the wife should not place herself in opposition to the hopes and efforts of her husband, though they be exaggerated, but express her opinion, and make suggestions, and then aid him what she can. Thus should the intellects of each correct the failings of the other, and make allowance for each other's erroneous views, mutually conceding a little, till both come nearly together, and unite in a correct judgment.

---

* I employ this form of expression, because it enables me to personify the organs, and thereby to embody and bring the full force of the idea presented and the principle illustrated directly before the mind in a manner more tangible and easily remembered than any other.

If Ideality be larger in the wife than in the husband, in all matters of taste, let her decision govern the choice ; and if Order be also large, see to it, that, on entering the house, you clean your feet, and do not carelessly make a grease spot, or soil, or displace anything about the house, lest you excite her anger, or permanently sour her temper.   In other words, do what will *gratify* this faculty as much as possible, and *offend* it as little as may be.   But let the wife remember that, if these organs be very large in her, she is liable to be particular, and make her " apple-pie order " cost herself and her family more than it comes to.

If your companion be frugal and saving, do not wantonly destroy even a paper, rag, or fragment of food, or incur any expense that is not *necessary ;* but take pains to gratify this faculty as much as is consistent, remembering that you thereby promote the happiness of your companion, and thus promote your own.

The application of this principle will be found a sovereign remedy—a real panacea—for all differences between you.   Try it.   That is, ascertain the phrenological developments of yourself and your companion, and then adapt yourselves to them by acceding and yielding to each other as the comparative size of the organs in each may require, and, depend upon it, it will only need an obliging disposition in you both to heal all differences that may arise.

If you ask " How does this principle direct me to conduct myself when my companion becomes angry," Phrenology answers :

Do not get angry yourself ; for this, instead of quelling his or her anger, will only excite it still more, and raise it into a hurricane of fury ; but just remember that it's only the momentary workings of excited Combativeness. Say nothing till your companion becomes cool, and then always address the higher sentiments.   This will produce repentance and reform.   Blaming the person will only make matters worse, and render you both more unhappy. " A soft answer turneth away wrath, but grievous words stir up strife." " Leave off contention before it be meddled with."   " Let your own moral sentiments dictate all your conduct towards them, and this will excite their better feelings towards you, and render both of you infinitely more happy than the opposite course.

Besides, your companion may be fretful or disagreeable, because worn down by labour, care, or anxiety in business, or because feeble or fevered in body. Physical indisposition usually excites the animal propensities, producing peevishness, irritability, a sour temper, unkind remarks, &c.   Such should be *doctored*, not *scolded*—they should be borne with and pitied, not blamed. Remember your *own* failings, and make liberal allowance for those of your companion.   Try the mild, persuasive course ; avoid collision ; and, on points of disagreement, " agree to disagree."   *Endure* what you cannot *cure ;* and, where you cannot attain perfect harmony of feeling, at least strive for peace ; and, if you cannot live together quite happily, live together as happily as possible.   Never, on any account, allow a harsh remark to pass between those whose relations are so sacred as those of man and wife.   Nor will this be often the case where *true* love exists, unless it should be caused by that fevered, irritated state of the body already mentioned ; for there is something in the very nature of love calculated to break down and subdue all minor points of disagreement, overlook defects, place the favourable qualities in their most exalted light, and produce a forbearing forgiving spirit.   And if those who are married do not possess this spirit and pursue this forbearing course, they do not really love each other.

Another important suggestion is to be careful about giving offence in small matters.   You cannot be too particular about little things.   So exceedingly tender is the plant of connubial love, and so susceptible of being lacerated, that even trifles impede its growth and embitter its fruits.   A single tart remark, or unkind tone of voice will penetrate the susceptible heart of a wife who loves you, and render her most wretched ; whereas, if she did *not* love you thus devotedly, her feelings would not be so easily wounded.

GRATIFY EACH OTHER'S FACULTIES.

That is, if your companion have any predilections in regard to food, dress, habits, friends, &c., not only should you pursue the indulgent course, but you should *assist* in procuring the desired indulgences. True, you should not go beyond the bounds of reason, or violate your conscience, or indulge any positively injurious habit ; but in non-essentials, and in matters of gratification merely, you should oblige and aid your companion as far as possible. If your wife insist on lacing your daughter tight, or on anything else that is wrong or hurtful in itself, it is your duty to resist such wrong, though it may place you and your wife in opposition to each other ; but, if she relish any little delicacy in diet, &c., gratify her appetite as often as you can. If she fancy a particular dress, do your best to obtain it ; if she love a particular book, or study, or pursuit, or amusement, not injurious in itself, do what you can to obtain it for her ; but never compromise *moral principle.*

In like manner, wives, also, can often gratify their husbands by cooking some favourite dish, or decorating a room, or playing or singing a favourite piece of music, &c., &c.

Let husbands and wives take pleasant rides, rural excursions, and rambles, agreeable promenades, and make visits together to their friends, as often as possible ; and let them hold frequent conversations on subjects of interest and importance to both, freely exchange views and feelings, ask and receive advice ; and, above all things, let them be open and frank. If you have committed errors, confess them and beg pardon ; and let there be no item of business, no hidden corner in the heart of either, into which the other is not freely admitted. Scarcely anything is more destructive of love than concealment or dissembling.

Another means is to read to one another, and entertain and instruct each other. Let the husband, while his frugal wife is sewing, or attending to her domestic duties, read to her from some interesting work, or explain something that will store her mind with useful knowledge, enlarge her range of thought, &c., and he will kindle in her breast a feeling of gratitude that will redouble her love, and make her still more anxious to be in his company. Let him make valuable suggestions, and aid her all he can in cultivating and exercising her intellect. As he comes in to his meals, let him tell her the news of the day, as well as matters of interest that may have happened to himself while absent. Especially let him be kind to her about the house in seeing that she has good fuel prepared at her hand, abundance of water, and all the materials and conveniences required in the family in good order.

Be kind and affectionate to the children also, and amuse them, and even play with them ; for, as the mother loves her children most devotedly, nothing will gratify her more, or more effectually promote her love, than seeing her children caressed. To make much of your children is to make much of your wife. Nor is it incompatible with the dignity of parents to play with and amuse their children. Indeed the relations between parents and children should be of the most familiar and intimate character, and calculated to endear them to each other. Austerity in parents is tyranny in its worst form. Be familiar with your children, and, as early as possible, let them become cheerful and welcome social friends in the family circle.

But there are some things which should not be done. Husbands and wives should never oppose each other in regard to the government of their children. Let there be a mutual understanding and agreement between them touching this point, and let a plan be concerted beforehand, so that the feelings of neither may be wounded by the interference of the other.

By doing and avoiding these and a thousand similar things may love be cherished and fostered till it takes deep root in the hearts of both, extend its fibres into every nook and corner of your souls, and imbues with its soft and endearing influence every look, word, and action. Practise these things, and those who even dislike each other at first (by thus removing the *cause*) may live together comfortably ; and two who do not positively cherish ill-will for each other, may render themselves *affectionate and happy.**

RENDERING NEIGHBOURS AGREEABLE.

A single remark, in regard to rendering neighbourhoods agreeable, and I close. Next to an affectionate family, an agreeable neighbourhood and good society become objects of desire. A contentious, tattling neighbourhood, where each is backbiting his neighbour, or indulging unkind feelings, is exceedingly annoying, besides souring the temper and lowering the tone of moral feeling. The amount and prevalence of neighbourhood scandal is really surprising ; nor are religious denominations exempt from its contaminating and unholy influence. This ought not to be so. The relations of neighbourhoods should be of the most friendly and accommodating character. Let village scandal be frowned down by every respectable citizen.

One of the best means of promoting good feelings among neighbours is, to manifest and excite public spirit, to form literary and other societies.

That this work may make more and better wives and husbands, and also improve the social and domestic condition of man, is the object of its publication and the ardent prayer of its author.

---

* There is another cause and remedy for disagreement between husbands and wives, mention of which, however important in itself, might offend, and therefore I pass it, with the remark, that I am preparing another work on a similar subject, to be entitled, "The Causes and Remedies of Perverted Amativeness," which. besides giving suitable warnings to the young, and disclosing an easy and efficient remedy for morbid or powerful Amativeness, will point out *one* cause of disagreement between husbands and wives, certainly not less prolific of discord and unfaithfulness than all others united, together with its easy and effectual remedy, as well as a perfect cure for both jealousy and unfaithfulness.

FOWLER'S WORKS

ON

𝔓hrenology, 𝔓hysiology, &c.

AMATIVENESS ; or, Evils and Remedies of Excessive and Perverted Sensuality. Including warning and advice to the Married and Single. By O. S. Fowler. Price 3d.

LOVE AND PARENTAGE, applied to the Improvement of Offspring. Including important directions and suggestions to Lovers and the Married. By O. S. Fowler. Price 3d.

MATRIMONY ; or, Phrenology and Physiology applied to the Selection of Congenial Companions for Life. Including directions to the Married for living together affectionately and happily. By O. S. Fowler. Price 3d.

PHYSIOLOGY—ANIMAL AND MENTAL, applied to the Preservation and Restoration of Health of Body and Power of Mind. By O. S. Fowler. Price 1s.

MEMORY AND INTELLECTUAL IMPROVEMENT, applied to Self-Education and Juvenile Instruction. By O. S. Fowler. Price 6d.

HEREDITARY DESCENT ; its Laws and Facts applied to Human Improvement. By O. S. Fowler. Price 1s.

FAMILIAR LESSONS ON PHYSIOLOGY. Designed to aid Parents, Guardians, and Teachers in the Education of the Young. By Mrs. L. N. Fowler. Price 3d.

FAMILIAR LESSONS ON PHRENOLOGY. Designed for the use of Schools and Families. By Mrs. L. N. Fowler. Price 6d.

INTEMPERANCE AND TIGHT LACING ; Considered in relation to the Laws of Life. By O. S. Fowler. Price 3d.

TOBACCO : its History, Nature, and Effects on the Body and Mind. By Joel Shew, M.D. Price 3d.

Vol. I., containing the above, neatly bound in Cloth, Five Shillings.

THE NATURAL LAWS OF MAN : A Philosophical Catechism. By J. G. Spurzheim, M.D. Price 6d.

MARRIAGE : its History and Ceremonies ; with a Phrenological and Physiological Exposition of the Functions and Qualifications for Happy Marriages. By Mrs. L. N. Fowler. Price 6d.

FAMILIAR LESSONS ON ASTRONOMY. Designed for the use of Children and Youth in Schools and Families. By Mrs. L. N. Fowler. Price 6d.

SELF-CULTURE AND PERFECTION OF CHARACTER. Including the Management of Youth. By O. S. Fowler. Price 1s.

MARRIAGE AND PARENTAGE ; or, the Reproductive Element in Man, as a means to his Elevation and Happiness. By H. C. Wright. Price 1s.

TEA AND COFFEE : Their Physical, Intellectual, and Moral Effects on the Human System. By Dr. W. A. Alcott. New Edition, Revised by T. Baker, Esq. Price 3d.

EDUCATION : Its Elementary Principles ; Founded on the Nature of Man. By J. G. Spurzheim, M.D. Price 1s.

MATERNITY ; or, The Bearing and Nursing of Children. Including Female Education and Beauty. By O. S. Fowler. Price 1s.

Vol. II., containing the last 8 Works, Cloth neat, Six Shillings.

Vols. I. and II., bound together, Cloth, Ten Shillings and Sixpence.

PHYSIOGNOMY ; or, How to Read the Character of Both Sexes at a glance ; wherein is Shown the Sure Way of Choosing Wives, Husbands, etc. By Dr. Jepson. Price 6d.

HEART MELODIES. A collection of Poems. By Mrs. Dr. Lydia F. Fowler. Now Ready. Price 2s., Cloth.

www.ingramcontent.com/pod-product-compliance
Lightning Source LLC
Chambersburg PA
CBHW021644270326
41931CB00008B/1167